I Wed Thee

together forever

Fr. Zygmunt Ostrowski, SChr

Cover design by Eluta Stańko-Smierzchalska and Wojciech Zebala
Illustrations by Eluta Stańko-Smierzchalska
based on photos Danuta Witkowska.

Illustration © Hlondianum Publishing Company, Poznań, Poland.

Translation: Anita C. Dolman and Margaret Olszewski

ISBN 978-0-615-61516-5

SGSI - *Concept, Design & Print*
Printed in USA

The Annunciation of the Lord
March 25, 2012

Ecclesiastical permission
Fr. Paweł Bandurski, SChr
Provincial of Society of Christ in America

Original Published in Polish as: Ślubuję Ci
Polish Editions: Gaudium 2007, Hlondianum 2008, 2010
Copyright © Ks. Zygmunt Ostrowski, SChr

English Edition
Copyright © 2012 by Fr. Zygmunt Ostrowski, SChr

Table of Contents

INVOCATION

It is to the greatest couple of this world,

MARY AND JOSEPH,

The most beautiful Virgin Mother and Queen,

The most faithful husband and guardian,

With deep admiration and gratitude

For their example of Faith and Love,

Their holy marriage and family life with Jesus,

Their Son and King of their united hearts and souls,

That I entrust and offer all

Engaged and married couples and families,

So that, joined together by the sacramental bond,

Two become and remain

One with the Lord.

Now and Forever.

Father Zygmunt Ostrowski, SChr

St. Joseph, Spouse of the Blessed Virgin Mary

March 19, 2012

Lombard, IL

A Word from the Bishop

Young people, on their road to independence, especially near the age where they can start a family, look for examples and models in the older generation: parents, cousins, uncles and aunts, and so on. Observing multi-generational family traditions, they are assured that their plans, life style, and moral norms are correct. They become accustomed to certain gestures, signs and behavior, especially in connection with those who are closest to them.

This social conditioning, or pedagogy, is especially important in relationships where emotions greatly influence human life. Here I have in mind specifically the relationship between a young man and a young woman. The natural process whereby young people realize that they are in love requires the kind of support from the adults around them that will help their love become the basis for a lasting life together.

In today's world, young people are offered many choices that are contrary to the tested ways of past generations. They are artificial, packaged in attractive media images, imported into various environments where young people come together, like schools or universities. These ways of living your life may even be supported by the "academic" authorities. They call upon statistics which point to changing ways and conclude that most young people choose a different path than that of the generation of their parents or grandparents.

Therefore, it is important to *accompany* a maturing young person on this path. It does not help to keep someone locked up at home. It would be even more difficult to constantly shield their eyes. The reality they face is so loud and infused into everything around them, that it is not possible to protect them from experiencing this new style of life. So, it is better to accompany them – be with them, advise them about what is an already tried, tested and true model of life.

To accompany means to serve, most importantly, with

the knowledge of God's truth. We all come from the mind of God; we are a permanent image of God and neither sin, nor cultural changes, nor any manipulation, be it the most malicious and effective, can cross out the works of the Creator. The design of God is the only true foundation on which to build a future family home. That is why we must know and serve this foundation first. Rather than moralizing reprimands or shallow encouragement to lead an honest life, we need to help a young person with a well understood and practiced "catechism" of married and family life.

Second, it is important to show them that certain values of family life never change and what permanently joins a man and a woman, making them parents, does not bow to the changes around them and statistics that are thrown in their faces every step of the way.

Third, we need to accompany them with faith that the good in a person is always stronger than his weakness. Human beings by their very nature are created to be happy, to do good and to feel they have reached spiritual fulfillment in the time they have here.

Fourth, we have to accompany the young person, loving them no matter who we are: priest, neighbor, friend or parent. Parental love given to the younger generation is the best way to pass on every truth, no matter how demanding it is. These are the expectations of educational academics, catechists, pastors, care-givers or any other persons who accompany young people on their road to creating their own home.

Into the hands of the reader comes this text by Fr. Zygmunt Ostrowski: *I Wed Thee...* I read this work while keeping in mind the above reflections about accompanying young people. The way I receive this text can be characterized by a subjective enthusiasm, due to the fact that I am connected as a brother in the Society of Christ – I was a teacher and Father Zygmunt my student. We have been friends since his studies in the Seminary, through his whole priesthood in Poland and among Poles abroad. Fortunately, my subjective opinion is confirmed by the carefully prepared opinion of this publication by Father Krzysztof (Christopher) Stola. I speak with gratitude about the author's opinion and in relation to it, I add my continuing thoughts about the work.

Father Zygmunt Ostrowski's text is first and foremost a fruit of his pastoral reflections. Our service as priests always requires great thought; however, we take every opportunity to become involved with the passing on of content. We take advantage of works that already exist. Father Zygmunt shares some very personal reflections of a pastoral priest with us. This text is a product of systematic study. Even though it is not an academic study, this private commitment to deepening the knowledge and supplementing the teachings of the Church can nevertheless be compared to the works written by those completing specialist studies. The reflections are filled with evangelical optimism that can also be found within the author himself. He sees the good in people, willingly helps in their development and is not discouraged by their weaknesses. Pastor and Father Zygmunt Ostrowski relates to his parishioners and people with love. He is always available and approachable thanks to the kindness he always shows in his relationships with other people. Due to this fact, he has had the opportunity to witness some of the most delicate and often hidden parts of human life. To approach all people with love and kindness is a specific aspect of Father Zygmunt's pastoral method.

There is still another circumstance to consider. This book originated at a time when Christ bestowed great suffering upon this priest. From being a very active pastor, Christ brought him into a new kind of ministry, whereby for many months he could only minster to the Church through his own passive suffering. He was constantly aware that he might never return to take up his full pastoral responsibilities, especially where good physical health was required. This dimension of God's presence in the author's life took on a special meaning, since it was necessary to continue serving in his pastoral duties while excluding the typical areas for us such as the pulpit and confessional. The altar remained, where in the quiet of everyday, Christ brings the grace of Salvation and as priests, with the permission of God, we place our own suffering there to be united with His.

The book *I Wed Thee...* may be used as marriage preparation material, as it supports the Catechetical teachings on marriage. It is written in such a way that it can be used *before* and *after* the wedding. Marriage preparation, we know from our experience as pastors, is often taken very superficially. It becomes a duty to be crossed off the "what to do" wedding list as quickly as possible. We know that family life, marriage and even the most personal reflections upon one's own relationships follow a constant process of maturing in faithfulness to God and in building communion with others. For this reason, the text prepared by Father Zygmunt may be excellent reading material for group meetings, for ministering to young couples, as well as for the older generation. The older generation should accompany the young married couples, although often times they themselves need support and advice.

This book can be a personal instructor in moments of silence and prayer before God. I am convinced that catechists and pastors who prepare meetings on various many different levels – from the confessional to formal marriage preparation classes – will take advantage of this very personal and Godly text.

God Bless all of you who take advantage of this enthusiastic and generous work of the author. May the Light of God and the joy of time truly well spent accompany you in your reading.

Stanislaw STEFANEK, SChr
Bishop of Lomza, Poland

Lomza, May 3, 2007
The Feast of Mary, Mother of God, Queen of Poland

A Word from the Author

Dearest Readers!

After the appearance of the Polish edition of this book, many people in the US and Canada asked me about an English language version. Therefore, I offer the English language version of this book for your critique. I hope it deepens your reflection on the great gift of God to humanity that is the Sacrament of Marriage.

This book is intended for engaged and sacramentally married couples, as well as those who care about them. Everyone will find something worthwhile among its pages. May this book help in your preparation to take up a life-long decision and discover the beauty of engagement and the Sacrament of Marriage. May it enrich the divine and human bonds within your engagement and marriage, and help parents in their conversations with their children.

The development of these gifts requires human dialog with God and mutual respect. Any heartfelt reflection upon the wonderful gift of this Sacrament will be helpful, not only for engaged couples, but also for sacramentally married couples. Though it is very difficult to change one's way of thinking and behaving after many years of married life, it is possible with the help of God and other people.

What you should not expect from reading these reflections:
- academic formulas, since I am a pastor, not a scientist;
- to be forced to read the entire book;
- a ready recipe for how to be a perfect person, how to have a perfect marriage and perfect family.

What you can expect:
- the necessity of "splurging" on some time for yourself to read and ponder;

- the possibility of discovering the truth about yourself, your engagement, marriage and family;
- an invitation to a difficult and creative collaboration, so that your lives together may be beautiful and that instead of ME and YOU, there would always be US.

What I expect from you:
- to find an even better book to read;
- to consider the declaration: "this is the kind of marriage I want to have";
- to enter into a more responsible way of experiencing your engagement and marriage.

What you can expect from me, a priest from the US and Canada:
- that I will share my pastoral experience and reflections;
- respect for your life decision of either YES or NO;
- permanent prayers of support.

You, my dear readers, I embrace with prayer in the intention of strengthening and renewing your married Sacramental life. May God help you realize your wondrous vocation to love in Jesus Christ. I thank you also for all your prayers in my intention as well.

I entrust you to God and the Most Beautiful Married Couple: Mary and Joseph. May they surround you with their care every day.

Fr. Zygmunt Ostrowski, SChr
Lombard, Illinois
May 3, 2011

The History of this Reflection

After being away from Poland for five years, I traveled there to bless Agata and Arek on the occasion of their Holy Marriage. After the wedding, I asked Agata to show me the materials their parish had given them to help them prepare for their Sacrament. After reading them I thought, "Do they want to make theologians out of you?" Furthermore, the three month waiting period required in Poland (6 to 12 months in the US and Canada) from the moment a couple visits their parish office is too short to adequately prepare for marriage. The engaged couples are already arranging the reception: the hall, the clothes, the invitations, the band, the menu, the photographer and so on. Then, they say they want a church wedding. At times, everything falls apart and there is neither a wedding, nor a reception. Where did their love go?

During my illness and lengthy recovery, I thought that maybe my reflections could benefit or assist someone in making the decision: YES or NO in regards to living in a Sacramental Marriage. I did not want to write a great big book - who would read it? I limited myself to the most essential topics and selected issues that are most important for engaged and sacramentally married couples.

The Sacrament of Marriage exists, but there is no Sacrament of Family. The more holy a marriage, the more holy the family. Children need their parents. It is the parents who teach their children through their daily example of love and sacrifice. Without great spouses and families there cannot be a strong society. The laws of the government in regards to marriage and family – the basic unit of society – are directed against their own people.

I was encouraged to write my reflection by: Krystyna (a lawyer and mother of four adult children), Dr. Elzbieta Kasjaniuk (from John Paul II Catholic University of Lublin) and Father Miroslaw Gebicki, who saw the need for writing a practical book in the Polish language. I thank them for inspiring me. I want to thank my professor Bishop Stanislaw Stefanek, SChr Bishop of the Lomza diocese and the Provincial Father Pawel Bandurski, SChr for permitting me to publish the first English edition, and theological advice of Father Dr. Krzysztof Stola.

After the appearance of the Polish editions of this book, many people in the US and Canada asked me about an English language version. This translation is the fruit of the work of two people: Margaret Olszewski and Anita C. Dolman. I thank them for their work.

Initial Preparation for the Sacrament of Marriage: Being Raised in a Family

You are not the only one who asks why we need preparation for the Sacrament of Marriage. Many say, "We are adults, we know what we are doing, we have worked out many differences before, we have the same ideals about life, and most importantly – we love each other!" That is beautiful, however, I do not think it would hurt you individually or as a couple to think through some additional topics related to the Sacrament of Marriage. As it turns out, the incredible feelings you share and all of your discussions are not enough to pull you through the engagement period, let alone marriage!

Stop for a moment and take a look around you. You may notice that a sincere desire and the deep conviction that "we love each other" is not enough. Taking the best driver's education course is not enough to be a good driver and never have an accident. A driver's license allows you to drive, but it does not force anyone onto the road. We drive when the need arises, at a particular time, the planned distance and we avoid driving during certain weather conditions.

Similarly, a marriage preparation course prepares you to enter into the Sacrament of Marriage, but it does not force you to. Furthermore, a marriage is for better or for worse – for always. So should you back away from the Sacrament because of its high demands? God forbid! I think it would not hurt to pause for a moment and think about this decision (maybe the most important one you ever make), which will touch the deepest experiences of your life here on earth and will have consequences through eternity. I am sure you will agree that it is worth spending a little time now, to gain a PRICELESS TREASURE later.

Marriage is the freely accepted responsibility to be TOGETHER - giving 100 percent - until the death of one of

US, seven days a week, 24 hours a day. Often times the US continues even after the death of one of the members of the marriage. Isn't that crazy? For some people, yes - for others, no. Every true love, where two people are just crazy about each other, is a kind of unique "madness" in the eyes of others, but not those who actually love each other. The saints lost themselves in their love for God.

For example, St. Paul, apostle of nations, wrote: "*I live, no longer I, but Christ lives in me*" (Gal 2:20). Maria, the sister of St. Teresa of the Christ Child, told her directly: "You are possessed by God" (September 16, 1896).

Remember: every authentic love must BE THE LOVE OF GOD! Only He is the source of all love. A human being did not discover it. The ability to love and receive love was given to us as part of our makeup from our Creator, the God of Love (1 Jn 4:16).

Now, to get to the point: your initial preparation for the Sacrament of Marriage is already behind you. It began even before you were conceived and continues until now, whether or not you are aware of it. It began with the lives of your parents and even earlier. You are the heirs of past generations. However, do not blame those who came before you for everything that is wrong, especially your weaknesses. You are one of the links in a chain of family, national and human traditions. You carry both good and bad, old and new within you. You are not responsible for their past. As your level of awareness grows you become more and more responsible for yourself and your own decisions. Persevere and be brave. Do not be afraid of yourself. Learn your own IDENTITY. Be yourself every day and then, you will mature and become ready to make responsible decisions.

Your childhood and adolescence have already passed, but sometimes you have to return to those times to find the answer to questions about your identity: who are you? There, you will find a lot of unexpected answers.

If, when you were a child, you had parents that loved and

respected each other, you are lucky indeed. Their example of sacrificial love toward one another as husband and wife, and toward you as the children, created the climate you needed to develop properly into young men and young women. Your father gave you your first lesson in manhood. Your mother, being respected by your father, her husband, taught you about womanhood! Growing up, you did not have to be embarrassed to be brought up in such a family.

By living the Sacraments, your parents showed you the importance of the Sacramental presence of Jesus Christ in their married life. Christ joined them even more closely during each Holy Mass and came into their hearts to enrich their everyday love, sometimes calling for great sacrifice and renunciation.

Remember that each person has both female and male traits! This fact should not surprise you. There is no person who has only male or female traits. Of course in a man, the male characteristics dominate while in a woman the female characteristics do. These characteristics should complement each other, rather than exclude the other. One needs the other. The key is their balance (dynamic, harmonious and a constant fine-tuning which is necessary for everything to work the way it was meant to) so that the man and the woman can be normal, well-balanced people of good character. It helps men to respect women and women to respect men. It allows them to enjoy their differences and accept them with understanding. It helps to build long lasting relationships between men and women, especially in marriage.

It also gives us a greater chance to develop our human potential to its fullest and helps married couples achieve much desired everyday peace and happiness. Such people of good character are a gift to society at large. They have been given a valuable gift – experiences they can tap into to get through difficult moments, because ordinary life carries great difficulties and challenges for us. Life on earth is not strewn with roses, and even if it were, roses have thorns.

Be grateful to God and your parents for the immense

richness of good that you have taken from your home. Remember your loving parents. If your parents are alive, thank them – together with your fiancé – for your beautiful upbringing, the wonderful son or daughter they raised and for your future husband or wife. If both of you come from families like this, I congratulate you! What a wonderful opportunity lies before you! What a blessing it is to be able to meet someone who comes from such a similarly beautiful background as you do. It is a great joy for a priest and the parents to see an engaged couple like this at the altar. It is a great grace from God, for the parish, society and the nation.

It is difficult for me to find the right words of compassion for those of you who grew up in completely different or even tragic circumstances. You carry great, unhealed wounds in your hearts. You may often have difficulty understanding yourselves, let alone another person. You are going to need help from God and those closest around you, from good and faith-filled psychologists or priests. Remember: do not throw your painful past under the rug, pushing everything into the unconscious. You have to name things for what they are. Do not run from the past, but experience it once again so that with God's help and that of other people – you can put it behind you once and for all! I warn you, however, that it is a painful process to name things for what they are in order to close those chapters of your life. I know this from my own experiences, from my pastoral work in Poland and North America. Do not hide your past from your fiancé. Masks that are donned during the engagement period quickly disappear once you are married. Then the tragedy is multiplied by many more people. I beg you: do not allow this to happen. It is easier to live with the truth than with a lie. You do not lie to yourself. Therefore, do not lie to one another from the start of your road together. You have to prepare yourself internally to be able to discuss the difficult and painful parts of your life. To stand in the truth, prepare yourself through prayer, so that you can truly discover who you are. Reveal your difficult past to your fiancé wisely and slowly. Their acceptance and understanding of your pain will be a sign of their love for you. It could be the first serious test for both of you. In moments like this, your old self may be revived, however, may the positive result of such an internal transformation be a new person (Eph 4:22 and Col 3:9).

Your adolescence was an especially important time of preparation for marriage. During this period, for the first time, you should ask yourselves these fundamental questions: Who am I? What is the purpose of my life? Who do I want to be? Who should I be?

A person's biological development often supersedes his psychological one. Girls develop faster than boys. Nature points girls in the direction of motherhood and caregiver, while boys are led towards fatherhood and the role of protector of his wife and children.

The development of psychological sexuality is different in a girl than it is in a boy. Boys often see a lack of sexual activity as a lack of manliness. This can lead to an inappropriate, fearful attitude or reckless "overcompensation" without taking responsibility for the consequences - both signs of immaturity and weak will. A girl, who does not accept her femininity or sees herself as less important than a man, will try to imitate a man's attitude and will try any method to be accepted by him. She will try to keep him by her side at all costs, even through sexual intercourse, turning herself into a victim. Then, she will be treated as an object to be used and will destroy within herself any possibility of full personal development and the ability to take responsibility for her own actions.

Keep in mind that the liberal media is not conducive to raising young people in chastity. It profits from advertising anti-conception and propagating the slogan, "You are free, so you can do what you want." It does not mention the consequences, however. The young generation, raised in this overly erotic world, is easily influenced by the media's propaganda. Young people, left on their own, find it hard to be themselves without smoking, alcohol, drugs or sex. They do not realize the price they will have to pay later. It is no wonder that when such an "unconstrained" and "free" young person meets a boy or girl that says "NO" to the proposition of sex or drugs, he is surprised and, in order to hide his own weak will, attacks or ridicules that person as being old fashioned.

Has anyone ever counted all the young people who have gotten burned by premature relationships? Has anyone ever counted all the people who have become enslaved by this liberal, "free" style of living? Young people, instead of searching for ideals and positive role models to help them to develop their character, become a burden to themselves by allowing for the deformation of their emotional, sexual and psychological development. Rather than respecting the richness of masculinity and femininity within themselves and in others, they destroy it, and afterwards - which is most tragic - some brag about their success of adding "another notch to their belts."

A young woman experiences her relationship with her boyfriend with more emotion and depth than he does. She, by her nature, loves with her whole being and immerses her whole world into the relationship. Therefore, it is not surprising that she will experience difficulties during an engagement or a breakup with more bitterness. Afterwards, she may be overly cautious and have difficulty establishing another relationship. If she feels hurt, emotionally crushed or morally violated, she may seek revenge on another undeserving boy or man she meets. Young men may behave similarly if they are cruelly rejected by the young woman they love.

At the end of this chapter about preparing for marriage through your own family upbringing, I want to mention the influence that your siblings have had on your psychological and spiritual development. These natural family bonds have shaped you. The joyful or painful experiences you have had with your family have positively or negatively affected the way you see relationships with others. Sometimes they slowed, obstructed or even derailed the development of your identity as a boy or a girl.

The situation is more difficult for you if you were raised as an only child. The whole world revolved around you! You were the center of your parent's attention and this could have caused a distorted view of self-love to develop; you may have become egocentric and egotistical. I think you missed having other children in your home on a daily basis. Just as damaging is the favoring of one child over another by one or both of the parents in families with many kids. A well-known example is that of Joseph in the Old Testament. His brothers, because of their jealously that their father loved him - the youngest son - most dearly, first wanted to kill him and ultimately sold him to merchants traveling to Egypt (Gen 37:3-28).

At this point, it is important to mention that the relationships you had with your siblings influence your relationships with your friends; your relationships with your parents influence your contacts with your superiors at school or work; and your relationships with your grandparents influence your behavior towards other older people. The more sincere and warmhearted the atmosphere was in your home, the easier your relationships will be with others outside of your home. Think back to your childhood home and thank God for your parents, brothers and sisters. With them and with their help, God has sculpted the interior of each of you. They were a chisel for you in the hands of the Lord as you were a chisel for them. Think of them with gratitude, but if they were not good to you, then try to reconcile with them – first in your own heart through prayer and forgiveness, and later directly with them, while they are still alive. Do this for your mutual psychological and spiritual good. A spirit of hatred and revenge destroys a person internally. Words of a song come to mind: "The world moves towards a great abyss, because a brother hates a brother." Indifference destroys one's life and relationships with others, leading them to conformity and egoism.

Remember that your positive family relations should continue, and with the coming years your relationships will become more important to you and more mature. Life enriches these relationships with various experiences: work and family related, intellectual, spiritual, emotional, and so on. I think you will continue to need your family and you will be able to count on their support. At family gatherings – often with a smile and without offense – it is possible to reminisce about difficult times as well as the more joyous moments.

The American National Anthem ends with these words: "God bless America, my home, sweet home." Frank Sinatra sang a beautiful song at the rededication of the renovated Statue of Liberty (a gift from France) entitled, "The House I Live In." The lyrics describe the wonderful things about daily life, the land and people of America. "The house" is a metaphor for country. No country is perfect, but your family home is the closest "country" to your heart. It is the cradle of your spiritual homeland, regardless of what it is called or how far away you live from it.

Remember, the examples you observed while growing up in your own family will make an impact on your own marriage and family. Maintaining positive family relationships will help you build similarly sensitive and fully committed bonds with other people, friends, your fiancé and later, your spouse. Your engagement and sacramental marriage are an amazing state of mutual and exclusive love, filled with the affectionate love of God and others. There is no room, therefore, for indifference or hatred, especially toward parents, brothers or sisters. Psalm 133 states: *"How good and how pleasant it is, when brothers dwell together as one! ...there the Lord has decreed a blessing, life for evermore!"* (v. 1, 3). Return to your original nest physically and spiritually, even with your entire families. These visits will strengthen you, helping you to become a better family man or woman. May the family spirit from which you have come and which you are now creating in your new life, be filled with God's love, just as He joined the Holy Family in Nazareth.

A Moment of Reflection and Dialog

1. Think of your family, about the positive and negative experiences you remember.
2. Who had the greatest authority in your family and why?
3. Who were your grandparents? Parents? Siblings? And what were they like?
4. What kind of memories do you have? Bring to mind both joyful and painful moments.
5. Are you ashamed of your family or are you proud of them? Why?
6. How do you remember the relationship between your parents as husband and wife?
7. What would you like to bring into your marriage from their lives, to change, to keep out?
8. Pray for your family:
   - thanking God for your parents, siblings, and relatives;
   - asking for God's forgiveness for any wrong that happened in the past;
   - asking God to help specific people: parents, siblings, etc.
9. Do you still pray for your parents, siblings, teachers, coaches, friends, priests and nuns?
10. Has someone hurt you? Have you forgiven this person? If not, then why?
11. Have you hurt someone during that time in your life and why? Have you asked for forgiveness and made up for your wrongdoing?
12. Write a prayer of closure for that time in your life - a prayer of forgiveness, thanksgiving and petition.

Preparing for the Sacrament of Marriage: The Engagement

Before you are engaged, you should examine your hearts, which are pulsating with feelings of joy and hope, and ask yourselves: Why do I want this man to be my husband? Why do I want this woman to be my wife? In trying to answer this practical question, engage your heart and mind, your feelings and intellect, as well as your faith, keeping intact your individual approach as a man or a woman. This process of discernment should accompany you throughout your engagement and marriage. Your different points of view will enrich your journey together. Your decision regarding your engagement and marriage should be a fully conscious and free choice, made by each one of you individually, never forced upon you by anyone. It should be a completely personal choice.

Pope John Paul II, in his Apostolic Exhortation *Familiaris Consortio* writes that, "The very preparation for Christian marriage is itself a journey of faith. It is a special opportunity for the engaged to rediscover and deepen the faith received in Baptism and nourished by their Christian upbringing. In this way they come to recognize and freely accept their vocation to follow Christ and to serve the Kingdom of God in the married state. The celebration of the sacrament of marriage is the basic moment of faith of the couple. This sacrament in essence is the proclamation in the Church of Good News concerning married love. It is the word of God that "reveals" and "fulfills" the wise and loving plan of God for the married couple....The discovery of and obedience to the plan of God on the part of the conjugal and family community must take place in "togetherness" through the human experience of love between husband and wife, between parents and children, lived in the Spirit of Christ." (51).

1. Goals and Tasks During the Engagement

Engagement is a specific time to:

- get to know yourself better, who you are, your good and bad points (this takes great effort), and then get to know your fiancé (if you consciously want to be responsible for this person before God and other people);
- discuss how you will help each other to continue your personal development;
- learn a dialog of the mind and heart, which is based on respect and truth, in order to deepen your love for each other;
- get to know the family of your fiancé (which may unexpectedly answer many hidden questions);
- discuss the most essential subjects for both of you, including your life together in a marriage and in a family. This requires great sensitivity and seriousness as it concerns the shared responsibilities you will have for each other until death separates you;
- talk about your sexual life and your life in chastity together – during your engagement and in your sacramental marriage; this leads to an understanding of this great gift of God, as well as, a respect for it now and in your future life together;
- discuss what role God should play in your individual, engaged, and later married and family lives. Faith and the mutual practice of a sacramental life with the goal of salvation for both, allows God to play a central role in your lives;
- undertake a responsible decision – to pray with God as your witness - that you want to be with this person until death (in spite of modern liberal laws that allow for divorce and the attitude that: "if it doesn't work out, we'll go our separate ways";

- discuss your marital finances and make realistic decisions which will demands sacrifice and discipline;
- visualize your free time together (vacations, cultural events, being together at home, out as well as with children;
- learn to converse as well as be silent with one another (God not only gave people the gift of speech, but also the beautiful gift to listen, a mysterious key to understand your own self as well as another person);
- demonstrate faithfulness in your feelings, attitudes and words;
- approach the other person's intimacy and sexuality with respect (faithfulness to God and each other); sexual activity during the engagement is not proof of your love.

It is very important to talk about these and other related issues. These conversations help you to get to know yourself in the presence of and during discussions with the other person. These discussions should not only take place during official meetings. Visits to your fiancé's house announced shortly before arrival will likely shed light onto many hidden aspects of your fiancé and his environment.

The engagement period should be a foretaste of marriage with the exception of sexual activity. Allowing for sex to occur during the engagement period shows a lack of respect for the commandments of God as well as for your own and the other person's sexuality. What will happen afterwards, during the marriage, if one or both sides do not show respect for one another now? Will respect for the intimacy of the other person remain? Friendship and sacramental marriage are not built through the bedroom. Sexual intercourse before marriage is a sign of a false understanding of love. God and His Law must be present in every love, so that we may attain the ultimate goal in life: salvation. How many women and men have been deceived during their engagements! How many children are left behind, even murdered through abortion, after this kind of sex!

Engaged couples should talk about the difficulties and problems that they may to encounter during their married life. One problem might be certain great differences between them, such as in: age, level of education, family traditions, faith and religion. Later, these differences will become obstacles to good marital relations.

A large difference in age can create a relationship that is more like that of a father and daughter or mother and son.

Marriages of mixed faiths encounter other difficulties, where the spiritual and psychological differences can sometimes grow so large that they are almost impossible to overcome. The Catholic Church can allow such marriages (the Catholic side can receive the holy sacraments). The Church, although granting permission, requires the non-Catholic party to affirm that he or she will allow their Catholic spouse the freedom to practice their faith, as well as baptize any children in the Catholic Church and raise them as Catholics. The Church, before granting permission, cautions the Catholic about the risk of losing his or her faith. The granted permission, however, does not resolve the problems such a couple may face. In mixed marriages, problems involving religion, different mentalities and traditions often appear after the wedding, especially with the coming of children who need to be baptized and raised as Catholics. Then the non-Catholic spouse can change his or her mind and say "no." What happens then? The first sign of potential problems is when the non-Catholic demands (often successfully) that the wedding not be held in a Catholic Church.

Other problems may appear when certain problems are hidden, such as: a physical or psychological illness, addictions (alcohol, drugs, gambling, expensive hobbies, the internet, computers and gaming) or even workaholism. Sometimes these hidden secrets can become the grounds for an annulment of the sacrament of marriage.

Parents should talk about these kinds of problems with their growing children, so when looking for their future spouse, they can make a smart, well-grounded choice that will truly make them happy. When your grown child brings someone home and introduces them as their future husband or a wife, it is too late to say (with surprise and pain): "we do not agree with your choice." Of course, there may be an exception to the rule, but is it worth risking your happiness not only in this life but your salvation as well? It is important to have serious conversations with your children so that they give great thought to who they should establish the kind of close relationships with that may lead to engagement and marriage.

The engagement is a wonderful, dynamic and creative time meant to learn how to express your own feelings (boys and men often have more difficulty in this regard), as well as your opinions about various topics, both moral and religious. It is a time to consistently demonstrate respect for the gift that the other person is for you, who they are and the appropriate boundaries of intimacy and sexuality.

The engagement is also a time to get to know both your positive and negative sides, as well as noticing them in your future spouse. It is a time to discuss these topics. Someone who is reluctant to talk about them raises suspicion that he is dishonest and concealing something. This lack of openness and trust is a sign of the person's inability to communicate, which is essential in a marriage. Authentic love is always open. It is demonstrated by the spontaneous help one person offers their loved one and the gratitude with which the other receives it. This is especially true in difficult, sudden and unexpectedly situations.

I do not want to dampen your moods during your engagement, but notice how many things need to be thought through and talked over in individual and joint dialogs with God. These should begin even before you choose your future spouse. Remember, only those engaged couples are truly happy who are in love with God and one another. Therefore, it is worth spending enough time to consider these matters before making the decision with whom to be with as a husband or wife, and later as a mother or father until death. Great maturity is needed to properly select the one person who is worthy of your exclusive love and for whom you will be responsible for the rest of your life.

2. Human Temperament

We will examine the important topics of **temperament**, in regards to a person's nature (like the soil), and **character**, which communicates their personal moral strength and development (to cultivate it).

a) The Four Temperaments according to Hippocrates (460-377 BC):

- Sanguine - optimistic, honest, joyful, social, polite, capable, brave, quick thinker, egoistic, volatile, sensual, weak-willed;
- Phlegmatic – slow to respond, persistent, honest, truthful, self-controlled, economical, lazy, consistent, reserved, stingy, unemotional, formal, overly critical, patient, faithful, sensual, peaceful;
- Choleric – explosive, passionate, argumentative, commanding, generous, enthusiastic, sure of victory, trustworthy, charismatic, dictatorial, confident, rebellious, applause-seeker;
- Melancholic – peace loving, serious, sad, noble, quiet, consistent in his feelings, a person of dialog, righteous, egotistical, penetrating, perfectionist, sensitive, stubborn, easily offended, not resourceful, shy, inclined to pessimism, compassionate, creative, a loner, undecided, dreamer

There are positive and negative traits in every temperament. This model is still relevant today.

b) Another 20ᵗʰ Century Classification:

- Excitable – sensitive, delicate, optimistic, joyful, sincere, weak-willed, inconsistent, talkative, entertaining, not enduring, vain, deceitful, impulsive;
- Dictator – power hungry, ambitious, sacrificial, hard working, self-controlled, tenacious, attains goal no matter what the cost, independent, conceited, violent, individualist;
- Volatile – a born artist, objective, obedient, attention seeking, lazy, sensual, extravagant, lacking ideals, undecided emotionally;
- Bureaucrat – lacking initiative, established, peaceful, serious, discrete, faithful, emotional, a loner, cheap, egotistical, robot-like, lacking in interests, resentful, stubborn, trendy, pessimistic;

This classification refers to both men and women.

c) Eduard Spranger's Classification of Personality Types:

Men:

- Theoretical (values culture, intellectual capabilities, not a homebody);
- Economic (values material issues, capable, comfort seeker, egotistical);
- Aesthetic (artistic, specialist of the arts);
- Political (wants to dominate over others no matter what the cost);
- Social (lives for others, sacrificial, a candidate to be a good father);
- Religious (seeks the meaning of life and its answers in religious values).

Women:

- Maternal (caregiver, needing to be loved, this is the most typical coming by nature);
- Erotic (likes to adorn herself, a coquette, does everything to gain every man's attention);
- Romantic (very emotional, yearning for adventure, a dreamer);
- Intellectual (the most important thing being all intellectual pursuits);
- Realist (homebody, conscientious, diligent, a good hostess, very capable).

It is interesting that Spranger, although claiming that spirituality appears in each personality type, does not single out a specific type for girls, even though girls are more spiritual than boys. During the engagement period and later in the sacramental marriage, spirituality is a crucial characteristic of both sides.

As personality theory developed, "classic" personality types were combined with "newer" ones and altogether, twenty-four new categories emerged. Today, some even conclude that there are as many categories as there are people. Regardless of the classifications, these characteristics teach us about the inner richness and poverty of each person. The positive traits create a wonderful human mosaic, whose Creator is God. It must be clear, however, that there is no ideal personality type; each one has its own virtues as well as shortcomings.

Every person is a unique individual - someone who cannot be copied. Each one of us has many temperamental traits which make up our personalities. Classification systems were created because certain traits tend to stand out. The number and diversity of these traits are somewhat of a problem for psychologists, since not every person fits into a narrow category. It is also important to remember that some people should not marry, since they possess certain traits that create problems impossible to overcome in marriage. Their relationships lead to divorce, since they cannot live with another person under the same roof. For a marriage to be successful, the spouse's traits have to complement each other. Therefore, young people should spend a lot of time to first, figure out who they are (their personality traits) and next, who they need (which personality traits compliment their own). Then, they can choose that a special person who will become their fiancé, and after getting to know that person better, their husband or wife. This is a difficult, but necessary process of learning about one another in order to make the right decision for an unrepeatable choice: ONLY WITH YOU until death.

3. Reasons for Choosing a Future Husband or Wife

- an acquaintance transforms into a romantic love based on a fascination with that person;
- the desire to live together in a Catholic marriage until death and to have a family;
- an impressive personality and character that is worthy of trust and which builds affection;
- common life interests, goals or hobbies, strong ties from school, university, clubs, etc.;
- a common desire to share a home and start a family (be wary of those who missed out on this in their childhoods; marriage cannot be an escape from an unbearable situation at home);
- fear of loneliness or a need to feel safe ("someone will take care of me");
- the prospect of increasing one's social status or material wealth (famous surname, riches, stable income, social recognition);
- gaining residency or securing citizenship in a country in where it is safer or easier to start a new life (especially in the situation of people who are materialistic in nature or immigrants trying to secure permanent residency);

- similar religious spirituality (membership in the same religious groups);
- the desire for a happy life (following the example of your parent's good marriage), etc.

A good foundation gives a marriage a better chance to last. Marriage for the wrong reasons, however, leads to the development of all kinds of problems, which often result in the breakup of the marriage. Not even a good reason can guarantee complete success and happiness. It is important to remember that a person can change, and his or her new attitudes are often impossible to foresee. Even the wrong reasons, if they are purified and true love is born from them, can lead to an enduring sacramental marriage. On the other hand, a marriage that started beautifully may be ruined by the egotism of one of the spouses, if he desires only his own way at the expense of his spouse. This type of situation may be bearable, but only for a time. How is it possible to foresee this? It is complicated, isn't it?

An interesting situation occurred in Barrie, Ontario, in Canada. One parishioner, born in Sri Lanka (former Ceylon), was asked to give her opinion about a young man who wanted to may her cousin in England. This young man traveled from England to Canada so that she could speak with him and pass her opinion on to her cousin. This is customary in Sri Lanka and India.

It used to be the same in Poland. Matchmakers played a momentous role. They came to the parents of a young lady in order to make a good match that would lead to an engagement and marriage. This was a highly respected and important function in the community. Obviously, the young couple did not always want to marry. Sometimes, the matchmakers would make a deal with the father of the bride, while neither the bride nor her mother had any say in the matter. What is most interesting, however, is that these marriages on the whole, lasted longer than the marriages of today which are based on a couple's "great love." Maybe it is strange, but according to statistics, true.

Dearest Engaged Ones!

Do not give in to the media's opinion that sex before marriage is a way to test your love. It is actually the opposite: a contradiction of the authentic love that you have for each other, a denial of your unity, and it may even destroy the most intimate communication of your feelings. It will surely not be an authentic union of hearts and love. The sin of premarital sex destroys a person's dignity and the foundations of their spiritual engagement and marriage. I remember reading, in catechetical materials I used in the 1970's in Poland that around 75 percent of civilly divorced couples stated sexual incompatibility as the reason their marriages failed. However, over 90% of those couples stated that they had sex before marriage. Therefore, what was supposed to be an expression and "test" of their intimate love and spiritual/physical unity ended up destroying their union. These are just the "dry" statistics. How much pain and tragedy lies hidden behind these figures: broken marriages and families, children without a home, without either a mother or a father!

Do not give into false information passed on through the liberal media that a lack of sex before marriage is not healthy and leads to disease. Let them prove these claims with medical research and not speculation! They will not because such medical proof does not exist! On the other hand, there is much medical evidence that sexually transmitted diseases and other negative results come with a liberal sexual lifestyle; this is not discussed, however, because this kind of lifestyle is very much in fashion.

Do not give in to the false information that you have to "try each other out sexually" before you get married, because this kind of "testing" is a sign of immaturity, as well as a lack of responsibility and self control. Premarital sex has caused many people pain and deception, leaving them without a marriage, while many of the children from these relationships end up being ripped out of their mother's wombs (murdered by abortion), or deserted by their father, mother or both.

You have probably heard many jokes about women who are virgins, but it is rare to hear about men being virgins. You may have laughed at these jokes, or even repeated them. However, these people, in our over erotic culture, are in a way, heroic. Chastity has never hurt anyone, yet sex outside of marriage has destroyed many, leading even to despair and suicide for many. Virginity brought into marriage is a truly great gift. Do not make fun of such a person, especially not your fiancé, but rather have respect for them. Mocking someone for this reason will hurt deeply and forgiving this injury can be difficult. Remember, this person displayed an enormous amount of effort and self-control to uphold his or her dignity and remain a virgin until marriage. You can be sure that this person understands responsibility. You can trust this person and depend on them, if you continue to treat him with respect. This person has worked with God for many years and has been faithful to Him. Similarly, he will be a companion to you throughout your engagement and sacramental marriage. Do not deprave him or you will both lose. Respect the presence of God in this person, and he or she will respect God's presence in you. With God, you will love each other with greater devotion.

Engagement is not easy, but it is a very creative time. It requires great effort. Do not waste this wonderful time. A successful engagement, besides helping you to get to know and develop yourself, also involves learning about your future husband or wife, and making many decisions that will help you when you enter into sacramental marriage. Living out the engagement in mutual respect provides the foundation to build a married life together that is based on respecting God presence in one another.

Before making a decision, you must ask yourself a very important question: not WHAT will I give my future spouse, but WHO will I give to him or her? Will I give myself completely or only some part of me? Which part of myself will I keep for myself and which will I to give? Will it be "a gift" or "a surprise" if my future spouse does not know me yet? Who or what will be in this gift? A person can only give himself completely, if he does not have psychological problems and is honest with himself and with others. What a person possesses, however, can be given completely or in part.

When you give yourself, you should remember that this gift brought into a sacramental marriage must be a gift in God. Each of you should be a gift in God. Remember this throughout your engagement and married life. When given in this way, you will be a priceless gift to the other person. God will help make this gift a gift of love, a gift of both the body and the soul filled with the living presence of God.

There is another important thing to discuss: your openness to life and to the upbringing of your children. Children "cement" a marriage because they are a gift of mutual sexuality in married love and in God, Who creates a unique and individual soul for each one of your children. You cannot "push" this aside for later, i.e., "let's live for a while and see". This is a vital issue, especially for women, who by nature want to be mothers and caregivers. A conscious and specific decision not to have children makes your marriage only an empty ceremony performed in a church, not a valid Sacrament of Marriage. The engagement period gives you an opportunity to discuss - the equally important - issue of children in your future marriage. There is a saying that although a child cannot lift a finger, it can keep a marriage together.

4. Emotional Wounds

An extremely important and painful topic is the internal emotional scars that a person may have. During your engagement, you should take note of their presence in one another and after admitting to them, begin the healing process. You may need someone to help you; if so, take advantage of outside help. Before you can reach this point, you must acknowledge the existence of these emotional wounds inside you, then carefully face and accept them, and finally, find the proper method to heal. A person who has been healed becomes more self confident and more sensitive to others. That person is more humble because he knows his own weaknesses and the difficulty of struggling with them. Do not pretend that nothing happened. Likewise, do not over exaggerate your wounds to play the role of the victim. Do not take another person's wounds onto yourself, but rather, show great compassion while keeping a distance and your objectivism. However, first you must help yourself and then others that are hurt. There are also those that hurt themselves and try to blame others (these types of people have a problems with the truth in their lives), but is that a loving and honest attitude in regards to the person you love?

Basic Types of Wounds

- Our own wounds – do not "reopen" them, but hope for healing and be cautious not to hurt others;
- Wounds caused by mothers – are very painful and can lead to addictions and obsessive behaviors intended as a "substitute" for her;
- Wounds caused by fathers – very painful and may lead to "absence of a backbone" (your own identity), lack of self-acceptance and adopting strange ideologies in place of him.

Different Ways to Help Heal

- Through God (the Holy Sacraments: the Sacrament of Reconciliation heals wounds; the Eucharist, after the experience of being unloved, abused or unable to love, helps us to trust in Jesus and accept His Forgiveness and Love); we must offer our wounds to God and ask for His healing;

- With the help of people (especially our family, friends, priests, psychologists and psychiatrists); I strongly recommend people who have themselves, in their hearts, reconciled with those who hurt them - they can be most helpful.

Different Ways of Healing

- From feelings of:
  - Sadness: do not feel sorry for yourself, but rather be sensitive to your sorrow so that you can gain a deeper understand of yourself;
  - Aggression: do not react violently when you are under stress; instead, find peace in your heart for the one who hurt you and build a system of defense against any further damage;
  - Indifference: stop being dissatisfied with everything, instead, try to find the joy in every situation and share it with others; try to see the hidden meaning in everyday events; this will help you to better know yourself;

- From passions that are:
  - Lustful: maintain moderation in food and drink, over stepping in these areas conceals a longing for (sinful) pleasures and eroticism;
  - Emotional: avoid "sexual opportunities" and solve difficulties in noble way (sublimation) - although sexuality may be a longing to "feel one's self" and a source of dynamic personal growth, nevertheless, it is important to remember that only God can fill the heart of a person who thirsts for a beautiful love, because He is Love - sexuality needs to be spiritualized and then it can help lead a person on the road to true happiness;
  - Spiritual: avoid them at all costs; know that passions are the source of many weaknesses and deadly sins, even

madness or demonic possession; remember that jealousy and pride will blind you;

- From internal strife:
  - Heal yourself by living a well-ordered and tidy everyday life;
  - Develop yourself in every personal situation in your life;
  - Accept yourself as you are (know your strengths and weaknesses – your own identity);
  - Work to better yourself, so that you can live in greater unity with God and other people;
  - Have an unceasing contact with God who is hidden in you, and with Jesus who is present and active in the Holy Sacraments, especially in the Sacrament of Reconciliation and the Eucharist, so that you will be able to experience the healing Love and Mercy of God;
  - Do not throw yourself into a whirlwind of activity to suppress the helplessness and anxiety that is in your conscience. Even after many years, it will surface with double the strength in a person who is internal scarred and lost; this can lead to despair and tragedy.

A Moment of Reflection and Dialog

1. Consider what kind of temperament and character you have, and which traits you must work on.
2. What kind of wounds are you carrying within you?
3. Start the healing process – with the help of God, and if necessary, with the help of others.
4. Why do you want to get married?
5. What should you change in your approach to your engagement and marriage?

Next, reflect together and answer these questions:

1. Are you thinking seriously about being engaged and then married until death separates you?
2. Do both of you consider engagement and marriage to be "holy"?
3. Do you truly know each other? Is either one of you pretending in any way?
4. Who and what kind of values do you want to bring into your marriage?
5. Do you share what brings you joy and what drives you crazy during your engagement?
6. Do you openly discuss all things?
7. Do you discuss doubts about each other and the things that make you doubt or feel unsure about yourself and one other?
8. Do you like to pray and attend Holy Mass together?
9. Are you faithful to one other?
10. Do you pray for each other?
11. Are you truly sure that you should BE TOGETHER as a sacramentally married couple until death separates you?
12. Finally and very importantly: are you open to having a child or children and raising them in the Catholic faith?

To conclude these reflections, I recommend the prayer, *"For the choice of a good fiancé,"* found in Chapter V, Section E.
I also encourage you to write your own prayer asking for the grace to make the right choice.

Direct Preparation
for the Sacrament of Marriage

Direct preparation involves an intensive consideration of the issues relating to a sacramental marriage. Participation in certain marriage preparation courses can be difficult for some people, due to schedule conflicts; i.e. inflexible employers or a busy parish priest. Another source of frustration for engaged couples is that they do not always hear that what they would like to or should hear; often the presentation of the material leaves much to be desired.

I led marriage preparation courses for many years. On several occasions, I had difficulty accepting the reasoning of Polish immigrants who believed that because they had a high school "religious certificate," they no longer needed marriage preparation courses or meetings, because "the priest who ran the certificate program said so." I congratulated them on their certificate, but I also explained that they needed to participate in this preparation course because of their new life situation.

One couple actually called off their engagement after only the first session entitled, "Being human in your marriage"! The topics of the marriage preparation course given once a week in my parish were the same as the chapters of this book. Homework was also assigned.

Sometimes I worked with only one couple. However, I dedicated the same amount of time and attention to this couple that I would if I had more. I always valued the participation of the couples in the course and I admired the dynamic energy in their eyes and hearts. It was a wonderful time – once a week – for six weeks. I am not and never was an advocate of a one shot deal, like a weekend marriage preparation class. After the sessions, I sent the engaged couples away with assignments. I believe that the teachings and reflections were useful, as was the homework I assigned. I wanted them – who were all very busy

– to stop for a moment and breath in Christ, who wants to help them build a happy and permanent marriage and family.

An American girl of Irish descent who lived in southern Maryland (near Washington DC), sent me a thank you card after completing her marriage preparation course and wedding to a young Polish man. She thanked me for helping them to "stop" for a moment to think seriously about their approaching Sacrament of Marriage.

Despite various difficulties, try to participate in a "course" that is offered in a parish and take the time to think over all the marriage preparation topics as a couple. It is never too late to learn something new. All of this may be useful in your married and, God-willing, family life.

Occasionally, a Sacrament of Marriage is celebrated at the same Mass as the Baptism of the young couple's newborn baby. I led a celebration of this kind at St. Anthony's Church in Lublin (in the presence of a doctor of theology from KUL – the Catholic University of Lublin – and a student of theology from the seminary of the Society of Christ for Polish emigrants). Even in this type situation, the priest should have a positive approach to the newlyweds and encourage them to be responsible for their marriage and new family.

I know that this book will not exhaust the questions and problems that come with engagement and marriage. There is a large variety of literature available in books, libraries or on the internet about these topics, in many different languages. With this in mind, I want to suggest only selected topics reflect upon and to invite you, as an engaged couple or already married couple, to consider having a dialog with God, who is Love and who is the Creator of your soul. Be open to growing individually and together. Do not be afraid to cross the THRESHOLD OF HOPE of your sacramental marriage hand-in-hand with Christ and in Christ!

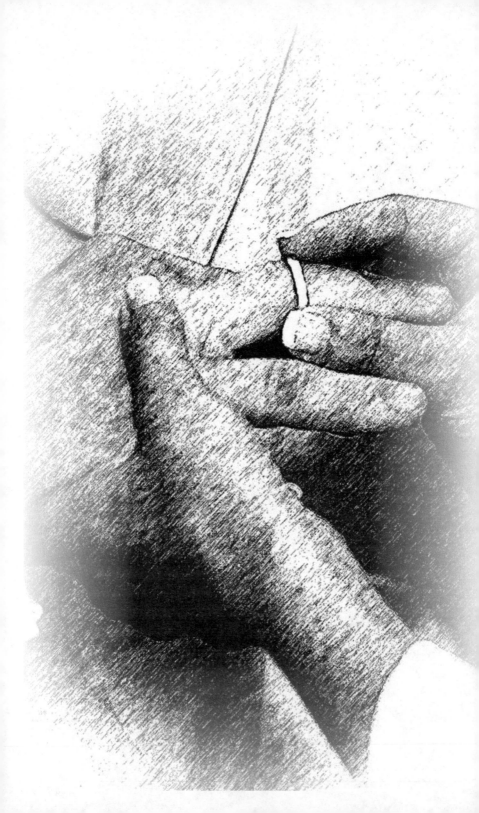

I. Theology of the Sacrament of Marriage

The call to marriage and family is a natural vocation for us. It is a gift that God the Creator gave to Adam and Eve. He created them to express the living image and likeness of God as they helped each other, procreated and became stewards of all the earth. The Sacrament of Marriage has three fundamental goals: love, fertility and holiness.

The pastoral constitution on the Church in the Modern World *Gaudium et spes,* from the Second Vatican Council, speaks of the holiness of marriage and family:

"A man and a woman, who by their compact of conjugal love 'are no longer two, but one flesh' (Mt 19:6), render mutual help and service to each other through an intimate union of their persons and of their actions so that just as He loved the Church and handed Himself over on her behalf, the spouses may love each other with perpetual fidelity through mutual self-bestowal. Authentic married love is caught up into divine love and is governed and enriched by Christ's redeeming power and the saving activity of the Church, so that this love many lead the spouses to God with powerful effect and may aid and strengthen them in the sublime office of being a father or mother.

For this reason Christian spouses have a special sacrament by which they are fortified and receive a kind of consecration in the duties and dignity of their state. By virtue of this sacrament, as spouses fulfill their conjugal and family obligation, they are penetrated with the spirit of Christ, which suffuses their whole lives with faith, hope and charity. Thus they increasingly advance the perfection of their own personalities, as well as their mutual sanctification, and hence contribute jointly to the glory of God (nr. 48).

Pope Paul VI, in his encyclical *Humanae Vitae*, 1968, wrote, "Marriage, then, is far from being the effect of chance or the result of the blind evolution of natural forces. It is in reality the wise and provident institution of God the Creator, whose purpose was to effect in man His loving design. As a consequence, husband and wife, through that mutual gift of themselves, which is specific and exclusive to them alone, develop that union of two persons in which they perfect one another, cooperating with God in the generation and rearing of new lives." (nr. 8)

The "Catechism of the Catholic Church" teaches us this about marriage: "From a valid marriage arises a *bond* between the spouses which by its very nature is perpetual and exclusive; furthermore, in a Christian marriage the spouses are strengthened and, as it were, consecrated for the duties and the dignity of their state by a *special sacrament.*" (nr. 1638)

"The consent by which the spouses mutually give and receive one another is sealed by God Himself. From their covenant arises 'an institution, confirmed by the divine law... even in the eyes of society.' The covenant between the spouses is integrated into God's covenant with man: 'Authentic married love is caught up into divine love.'" (nr. 1639) Thus, the marriage bond has been established by God Himself in such a way that a marriage concluded and consummated between baptized persons can never be dissolved. This bond, which results from the free human act of the spouses and their consummation of the marriage, is a reality, henceforth irrevocable, and gives rise to a covenant guaranteed by God's fidelity. The Church does not have the power to contravene this disposition of divine wisdom."(nr. 1640)

"'By reason of their state in life and of their order, Christian spouses have their own special gifts in the people of God.' This appropriate grace of the sacrament of Matrimony is intended to perfect the couple's love and to strengthen their indissoluble unity. By this grace, they help one another to attain holiness in their married life and in welcoming and educating their children.'" (nr. 1641)

"*Christ is the source of this grace.* 'Just as of old, God encountered his people with a covenant of love and fidelity, so our Savior, the spouse of the Church, now encounters Christian spouses through the Sacrament of Matrimony.' Christ dwells with them, gives them the strength to take up their crosses and so follow Him, to rise again after they have fallen, to forgive one another, to bear one another's burdens, to 'be subject to one another out of reverence for Christ,' and to love one another with supernatural, tender, and fruitful love. In the joys of their love and family life, He gives them here on earth a foretaste of the wedding feast of the Lamb...." (nr. 1642)

"Spouses to whom God has not granted children can nevertheless have conjugal life full of meaning, in both human and Christian terms. Their marriage can radiate a fruitfulness of charity, of hospitality, and of sacrifice." (nr. 1654)

Marriage and family were of particular concern to Pope John Paul II When he was still a Bishop, Karol Wojtyla wrote a book entitled *Love and Responsibility*, and later as Pope, he frequently lectured and wrote about the sacrament of marriage (for example, his *Theology of the Body* lecture series presented during his Wednesday audiences from 1979-1984). He also introduced the World Congress of Families, and it is not surprising that Family Institutes have already appeared in many countries. Marriage is, by its very nature, the foundation of family and community life, and as a domestic church it becomes the natural place for the development and sanctification of the married couple and their children.

In his apostolic exhortation *Familiaris consortio*, Pope John Paul II writes that: "...Christian revelation recognizes two specific ways of realizing the vocation of the human person in its entirety, to love: marriage and virginity or celibacy. Either one is, in its own proper form, an actuation of the most profound truth of man, of his being 'created in the image of God'. Consequently, sexuality, by means of which man and woman give themselves to one another through the acts which are proper and exclusive to spouses, is by no means something purely biological, but concerns the innermost being of the human person as such. It is realized in a truly human way only if it is an integral part of the love by which a man and a woman commit themselves totally to one another until death. The total physical self-giving would be a lie if it were not the sign and fruit of a total personal self-giving, in which the whole person, including the temporal dimension, is present: if the person were to withhold something or reserve the possibility of deciding otherwise in the future, by this very fact he or she would not be giving totally.

"This totality which is required by conjugal love also corresponds to the demands of responsible fertility. This fertility is directed to the generation of a human being, and so by its nature it surpasses the purely biological order and involves a whole series of personal values. For the harmonious growth of these values, a persevering and unified contribution by both parents is necessary.

The only 'place' in which this self-giving in its whole truth is made possible is marriage, the covenant of conjugal love freely and consciously chosen, whereby man and woman accept the intimate community of life and love willed by God Himself which only in this light manifests its true meaning. The institution of marriage is not an undue interference by society or authority, nor the extrinsic imposition of a form. Rather it is an interior requirement of the covenant of conjugal love which is publicly affirmed as unique and exclusive, in order to live in complete fidelity to the plan of God, the Creator. A person's freedom, far from being restricted by fidelity, is secured against every form of subjectivism or relativism and is made a sharer in creative Wisdom." (nr. 11)

"The sacrament of marriage is the specific source and original means of sanctification for Christian married couples and families: this gives rise to the grace and requirement of an authentic and profound conjugal and family spirituality that draws its inspiration from the themes of creation, covenant, cross, resurrection and sign, which were stressed more than once by the Synod. Christian marriage like the other sacraments, 'whose purpose is to sanctify people, to build up the body of Christ, and finally, to give worship to God,' is in itself a liturgical action glorifying God in Jesus Christ and in the Church. By celebrating it, Christian spouses profess their gratitude to God for the sublime gift bestowed on them of being able to live in their married and family lives the very love of God for people and that of the Lord Jesus for the Church, His bride. Just as husbands and wives receive from the sacrament the gift and responsibility of translating into daily living the sanctification bestowed on them, so the same sacrament confers on them the grace and moral obligation of transforming their whole lives into a 'spiritual sacrifice.'" (nr. 56)

The couple offers the Sacrament of Marriage to one other (with the priest as a canonical administrative witness), when they exchange their mutual, ceremonious vows of marital love and fidelity until death. For this reason, in full agreement with Church law, a valid sacrament can take place when, in certain extraordinary circumstances, a priest cannot be present as an administrative witness, but the couple, vows to one another to be together in marriage until death before God and other witnesses.

The following strange situation occurred in eastern Poland and later had its finale in Sterling Heights, Michigan. During the war, two young people vowed to be together as husband and wife before God and witnesses. A priest could not be present due to the extremely difficult war conditions. The young man joined General Anderson's army to fight for Poland's freedom. The young woman and her mother were taken to Siberia by the Russians. The young man lived through the war and ended up in the United States. He searched for his beloved through the Red Cross to no avail. He later married a Portuguese woman with whom he had two sons. After a certain time, however, the marriage ended in divorce. He remained alone. When his young love and her mother were repatriated into Poland, she immediately began searching for him and found him in the U.S. The war veterans in London helped her to locate him. She sent him a letter and he invited her to come to him. After she arrived, she declared with great determination that her marriage to him was valid, while his "second" one that took place in the church was not. The Marriage Tribunal in Detroit declared that she was indeed correct. During a Mass presided by Fr. W. Gowin, SChr, he explained these circumstances to their gathered friends. Then, for the first time in over 30 years they renewed their marital vows in front of a Catholic priest and received their first blessing for... a sacramentally married couple. Unfortunately, they were unable to enjoy their lives together for very long. He became ill with cancer. They moved to Florida (a better climate) and he died there. Their marital love helped them survive the horrors of war and the atrocities of Siberia, in order to finally stand together at an altar far from their own homeland.

Oh, how amazing is God in His gifts for those who, despite many experiences, endure faithfully in their married love.

II. Being Human

   The first fundamental question to consider and assignment to complete will be to discover your individual response to the following questions: Who am I? Who should I be?

   I do not want you to consciously look for an answer to the question: who do I want to be? I have met many people who tried to be somebody that they could never be, for example, because of a lack of a basic talent, like a good ear for music or feel for rhythm is necessary to a violinist or a pianist. I have also met many "big kids" with wrinkles and gray hair who collect retirement pensions. Always look for answers that are supported by the truth. It is possible to deceive others for a while, but not yourself. It is possible to hide your problems from others or run from them, but no one can run away from themselves or from the problems they carry within themselves. During this reflection, I try to stay away from learned concepts. There are many academic publications available in libraries and books stores. Choose books that are authentically worthwhile and that underline a person's relationship with God. Otherwise you might unnecessarily waste your time and money, and even worse – something of unequaled value – yourself as a child of God. We received the gift of childhood from Christ. It is He, who in the mystery of the Sacrament of Baptism, united us with the Holy Trinity. It was Christ who brought us into God's Family life. This is why being "only" human is not enough for us. We have to be children of God on this earth, and heaven should be the goal of our journey. We should do everything so that at the end of our pilgrimage, when we pass through the gates of death, we can go straight to our Father's House and stay with Him forever. We, the baptized, must never forget this. Through Christ we receive the dignity of being children of God and it is as if God's "holy DNA" was written into our souls. This gift determines who we should be and what the ultimate goal of our lives.

From the beginning people formed natural marital bonds as man and woman. Today, there is a vicious attack against the institutions of marriage, family, and especially the Catholic Church, who unceasingly defends sacramental marriage between a man and a woman. Liberal anti-Christian, anti-human communities lead well-financed, ruthless media and legal attacks to destroy the meaning of marriage as a union between a man and a woman, something that has been sanctified by God's law, as well as the age-long traditions of people and nations. To be human is to be not only a physical reality, but most importantly, to be a great spiritual reality, full of mystery; a mystery that is often misunderstood by the person himself. Immersed in daily life, a human being has no time to think about and consider the answer to the question, "who am I?" What is the ultimate goal of my life? Nevertheless, the most amazing living thing on earth is still a human being, who needs vivacious, dynamic relations with others and most importantly, with God – the Creator and Love itself.

1. Human Beings: the World's Greatest Miracle

The human being is a truly miraculous – though contaminated by his tendency toward evil (sin) – mystery-filled "union between body and soul." It was God (Love) who "designed" and created humans in His own image and likeness. It was God who created human beings as men and women. He called them to discover their capabilities and develop more fully through His Love – already now, so that they may remain with Him through all eternity.

A person's greatness is an incomprehensible mystery for which we must show respect and deep consideration. To be human is a wonderful, great gift and a tremendous task. It is not enough to just evaluate the "outward appearance" of a person, but one needs to get to know and appreciate his or her inner being. You have to open not only your eyes and ears, or feel that person not only with your senses, but most importantly, open your heart and soul to recognize him or her as a great miracle. Only through your heart can you discover God and another person.

Pope John Paul II, during his first pilgrimage to his homeland, spoke out these words in Victory Square, Warsaw (June 2, 1979): "It is not possible to truly comprehend man without Christ. Rather: man cannot truly understand himself without Christ." Oh yes! It is Christ who through His redemptive death bore us into a new life with God. That is why man needs God, who, in His gift of love, gave him a soul capable of loving Him in return. It is "God's DNA" which separates us from other creatures, and its realization in God gives great witness to the Creator and to the greatest of His creations, which is the human being.

We should approach every human being with respect and love. This is the language of understanding and creativity among people. Marriage, as a union of love, is a wonderfully natural place for daily dialog and bringing new people to life, as well as a place for their development.

The liberal media often treats people perfidiously: bypassing God's presence in their lives or simply separating them from Him. There are two basic concepts of man: first, platonic (idealistic), second, materialistic. Today, advertisements force materialistic visions upon us, colored by eroticism and "plastered" with scantily dressed women and all their visible charms. Movies, songs, books, radio, television, as well as, the tabloid media further deform the image of men and women. The perversion of truth, which is practically satanic, often triumphs, leading to addictions and enslavements such as sex, alcohol or drugs.

Who can count how many people have lost their dignity through the influence of the liberal media? Who can study the number of shattered marriages and families? Do we know how many children and young people have been hurt and deprived of parental care? And how many people committed suicide because they could not find any further meaning in their lives? Has the liberal media ever announced the number of murders and crimes have been committed that mimicked scenes from movies and television, in order to gain notoriety and front page fame? Will the owners and creators of liberal programming ever answer in court for deforming the human person and society? They can hide behind the curtain of freedom of speech guaranteed by the democratic constitution of a country that is run by liberals, but they cannot hide from God or from their own conscience. How long will the media go unpunished and continue to unscrupulously count their ever increasing profits made off of human weakness and tragedy?

Humans cannot stand internal emptiness – they search for someone or something to fill that poor emptiness inside. Once in a while, you will hear stories about individuals who had it all: fame, money, media attention, power – almost everything and everyone at their service - but suddenly they come to realize that it does not give them happiness. They lose their purpose in life, close themselves off and sometimes commit suicide. A few of them experience the unimagined grace of conversion – and like the prodigal son or Mary Magdalene – they return to God after many years in a "distant land" of indifference, or even the struggle against humanity and God Himself. Some, however, remain irreconcilable until death itself. Do the owners of the liberal media have any honor at all, to admit to the damage that they have inflicted upon entire generations? Will they ever ask for forgiveness from God and the people? This is the world we live in – you and I.

Maybe this kind of propaganda has also made you feel free and independent from moral and religious values? This would be nothing new. Satan, who is presented in the Bible as a snake, is "not on vacation" and today continues to successfully tempt many, as he once tempted the first parents: *"you will be like gods, who know good and evil"* (Gn 3:5). Ask yourselves, whether you are truly free people?

I would be insincere if I did not remind you of the moral principles of the Catholic Church! I am convinced that you want to be happy in your own marriage. But, can you be immune to the liberal media? You do not have to look far to find what is your enemy and that of your marriage. Turn on the television or the radio, buy newspapers or books full of lies, listen to bad music or watch bad movies, visit unacceptable websites on the internet, and you will yourselves invite the enemy into your hearts and homes! The media did not create human beings. The media battles with God while "wearing white gloves," - systematically deforming and destroying human dignity. Oh, how little programming exists that supports the true good in people and gives them hope of finding happiness in God. Always seek the answers to these questions: Who is man? What is the ultimate goal of a human being?

2. Who is the Human Being as a Man and a Woman?

This very existential question has been asked and continues being asked by many scholars and ordinary people. Liberal propaganda still puts forth theories created by some "scholars," who proclaim theories of the animality of human beings due to their biological origins. These theories leave no room for logical candor in the face of our Creator and man. In eliminating God, as well as, casting doubt on the natural dignity and human rights of man, these theories have one goal: to use every available means to commit sacrilege, or to secularize man. In other words, to separate man from God the Creator and to lower him to the level of animals, albeit the most evolved of the primates. It is easy to manipulate and justify the behavior (even deviations) of this kind of human, as well as protect and legally shield him from punishment even when destroying others through abortion, laboratory experimentation (in the name of curing disease and future health) or euthanasia. In a secular culture which removes God from society, man becomes the ultimate norm for himself and his fellow citizens. This type of system has turned against man throughout history. The 20th century is filled with examples. Liberal governments in many countries pass liberal laws, including laws that give the right to eliminate the "uncomfortable" people in society (the most innocent and helpless such as the embryo, the fetus or the very expensive to care for, terminally ill or older person), projecting this policy as a normal and necessary practice. How very tragic that the legally protected life of a person can be, by that same law, and without any consequences, destroyed! Liberal and politically correct law approaches human life selectively. It also selectively protects the interests and ideologies of its lawmakers and politicians. Observing these tragically deviated laws, these questions come to mind: For whom is it so important to destroy humanity and human dignity? Where is the logic and truthfulness of politicians and lawyers? What guides those who write laws and force others to uphold them against natural law and the conscience of healthy minded individuals (doctors, nurses or medical laboratory personnel)? One thing is for sure, those who destroy others through various methods, will answer before God the Creator and Just Judge for their battle with Him and His most beautiful creative work, which is the human being.

Regardless of what other theories will be proclaimed, one thing is clear: a human being is a person who dynamically realizes his vegetative (similar to plants), sensual (similar to animals) and spiritual (intellectual and religious) life in order to establish a personal relationship with God and other people. The human being is the only creature on the earth that connects all these different "forms of life" and realizes himself by recognizing his own identity within himself, other people, God and the surrounding world.

The human being is the subject of various types of research: medical (the body and senses), psychological and psychiatric (thought, desire, intellect and will), historical (individual and social achievements), religious (spiritual capacity), as well as, philosophical (existence, nature, the meaning of the world and human beings). Man is the only creature on earth that is capable of knowing himself with the help of his mind and senses, defining himself as a person who is intelligent, free and loving. He develops himself by knowing and loving freely – as "SOMEONE." Man joins matter and spirit within himself. This is why you cannot limit and restrict man to the purely material world. Neither can you close him within a purely spiritual world. A comprehensive approach to the human person must encompass these two worlds – the physical and spiritual. Human beings are the shame and the glory of the universe: "a thinking reed," according to Blaise Pascal.

A person who acknowledges his dependence on other people should also recognize his dependence on God the Creator, who gave the human soul its "holy DNA" and other gifts needed for the realization of human identity in the image and likeness of God. Man, regardless of scientific progress, is still a mystery, even to himself, and that is why he needs Christ to know himself and make sense of his life.

Empirical sciences cannot completely understand nor explain the human phenomenon. We need theology – to see through the eyes of God. It is God who reveals Himself as the Creator of the human being. It is man, influenced by Satan – through disobedience – who desired to know good and evil as does God. Man lost not only his friendship with God, but also the original harmony of body and spirit. Jesus Christ, through His redeeming death on the cross, reconciled man with God, and through Baptism made him a child of God. Although after death, every person will live in eternity, for some it will be joyous, while for others, tragic. Christ left no doubt as to this in the Gospel.

Some people are very selective in their acceptance and interpretation of Christ's teachings. As "teachers of the people," they muddy people's minds through their access to the mass media, teaching according to their own ideas and by narrowing the objective vision of reality. They are false teachers and "prophets of their own agenda"! But man, in order to attain the goal that God has planned for him, must work together with Him on earth until death, and in the resurrection will regain harmony and eternal happiness.

A person's upbringing should take into consideration God the Creator and the dignity of the human person. It should also involve his mind and will, to come to know wisdom and freedom, **to** grow in truth and **to** do good while rejecting lies and evil. This kind of formation will lead to a person's full development and integration.

The Human being possesses a body and soul. People possesses a theoretical intellect that is capable of grasping the principle meaning of things, gathering knowledge and wisdom (being faithful to truth and goodness), as well as a practical intellect that reveals itself prudently (in its judgments) and directed towards good (morally). Using their free will, people reach for the good of creation in accordance with nature, supported by principles, knowledge and wisdom. The human body possesses both external and internal senses, that serve the soul (especially through intellect and will), in establishing a fuller understanding of and in making the right choices. Human morality, based on the Revelation and teachings of the Catholic Church, is wisdom directed towards truth and goodness, the connection between people and their conscience (the ability to make intellectual statements and the ability to use free will to discern between good and evil). The human has feelings (including lustful and irritable ones) that are tied to emotions, manifesting in the desire to discern between good and evil. A person can control his senses through his imagination, which is influenced by a specific judgment.

Human beings are responsible for their own actions because they can control their feelings, intellect and will. For one person to take responsibility for another, he must to get to know the other. This is especially true for engaged and married couples. The greater the love, the greater the knowledge of the beloved person. The greater the knowledge, the greater the responsibility.

Here, I would like to share with you an interesting and profound reflection by Phil Bosmans:

"A good person is always a grace for the world.
Be a good person!
Man, you are not created for production, nor industry, nor for a bank account – you are created to be a person...
You are created in the image of God – who is Love...

My eyes are given to me, so that I can notice others;
Ears, to hear them;
Legs, to hurry to them;
Hands, to support them;
and a heart, to love them.
My mouth is to distribute a good word, like bread, to anyone who awaits it, whereas, my lips, with a true kiss, declare my love, linking hearts devoted to each other.
Hands are given to me to delicately and wholeheartedly feed the poor with bread and consolation.
My heart is to love and with its affection warm those, who are lonely and who experience the coldness of other people's frozen hearts.
Everything has its purpose...
The most important thing in this world is to be human, and to be a good person...

Wherever love reigns, God is there.
The Love of God overfills me to the last membrane of my being.
I feel loved.
I am filled with gratitude, but tell me, whom I should thank.
None of the Presidents, nor generals, none of the professors nor technocrats.

I desire to thank only God, my Good God. He caresses me with a thousand hands. With a thousand lips, he kisses me. He feeds me with a thousand fruits. He lifts me with a thousand wings. He is my God. I am infinitely close to Him."

(P. Bosmans, *Byc Czlowiekiem,* Warsaw 1990, p.p. 10-17; German title: *Worte Zum Menschsein)*

3. A Person's Two Goals

A person's earthly goal encompasses every sphere of his life: his intellect, emotions, physical and mental health, religion, work, relaxation, entertainment and so on. Even though attaining this goal requires time and dedication, it is not only the visible and measurable success that defines a person. Defeats are also part of human growth. Lessons of human weakness should help people attain humility (the truth about themselves). St. Paul, the Apostle of the Nations, glorified his weaknesses. He believed that Christ strengthened him through His grace. A person must free himself from his own self in order to allow God and others to live "within". The more a person allows God and others live "inside" his heart, the easier it will be to attain his true purpose: eternal joy in the House of our Father. Death, no matter how painful it may be, is only a physical defeat. In Christ's resurrection, a person will experience the perfect triumph of God's Spirit within him. This will also be God's victory within that person. A person completely emptied of worldly faults and imperfections will be filled with the Glory of God. This is why every earthly goal that a person aspires to, needs to be directed toward his ultimate purpose.

The ultimate goal involves the entire life of a person: not only from conception through death, but even more importantly, afterwards. A person should always remember that his ultimate goal is to live with God in eternal love in heaven. Only God, who is Love, can ensure this kind of life. It would be good for you to remember this Latin phrase: "Whatever you do, do it carefully and look toward the end." A person's end is not death, but what is beyond: eternal life. Otherwise, human existence would be senseless. God created humans for eternal life with Him, not only to struggle through this world full of difficulties and suffering. Death, for humans, will be deliverance to eternal unity with God. You should not be afraid of death, therefore, if you live with the Lord every day. Rather, look forward to it with joy because it will lead you to God.

4. Who Should a Man and Woman be?

About men and women in general

Both men and women should be true to their nature and marital vocation, and open to the birth of a child, which will enrich their lives and make them a family. In today's world, some propose that people, marriage and society, in general, should be unisex, or without the sexual distinction of "woman" and "man". Laws are even being introduced for these groups of people. Still, it is impossible – even with equal rights – to abolish the natural differences between a man and a woman.

The physical differences of the body are visible "to the naked eye", without even taking into consideration psychological, biological, spiritual and other differences. The biological system of a woman has a great impact on her ever-changing cyclical cognitive and emotional life. These cyclical changes affect her behavior. Her husband should notice this and respect it. When a wife begins to behave emotionally (physical pain, aggravation, increased sensitivity and weepiness), then her husband should be more sensitive, affectionate and protective of her. A woman and a man have their own spirituality. The instinct to give and nurture life lies in a woman's nature. These issues are the most important to her. Male abstraction is foreign to her. It is in her nature to be a man's "life partner." She participates in every part of his life. Usually, women stand behind the great successes and failures of men. It is in the man's nature to surround a woman and children with responsible care and ensure their safety. However, we can now observe the tendency to move further and further away from this natural pattern.

A few fundamental differences and... threats

A wife, a woman, converses differently than her husband, a man. She focuses on details and she becomes a specialist in all of the smallest matters; she remembers everyone and everything. Very often, she lets her intuition guide her. Theoretical thinking is not usually her strongest point. She has a great desire to be heard by her husband. She desires not only to hear from him that he loves her, but also to experience it in everyday life. She does not understand strange male logic, which is full of abstractions. She concerns herself with making sure that everything is in order at home and everyone has everything they need. She is very hurt by criticism of how she runs the household and cares for the children, especially by those "who don't lift a finger" to help. In moments of crisis, she is tortured by her husband's nonchalant remarks: "Don't worry, everything will turn out somehow; everything can be fixed...," and so on. Worried as she is about everything and everyone in the house, at times, "she forgets to eat or sleep enough," while taking care of everything else. She finds herself in helping others: she chauffeurs the kids, does the shopping and takes care of everyone. Tired to the point of exhaustion, she needs time at home to rest a moment and her husband's arms around her to feel safe and loved. If she feels hurt, she "falls to pieces." When she talks, she needs a listener and while she speaks, she discovers what she wants to share. An impatient husband may often not want to listen to her "female chatter" because what she really wants to say comes at the very end of her outburst, which drives him nuts! A wife should also remember not to play the role of a victim when sharing with her husband.

The husband, a man, only speaks when he has something specific to say, when he wants to communicate something to his wife. His silence is not a sign that he does not love her. A man is not much of a talker when it comes to certain subjects. A man's mind thrives on synthesis and the abstract; he is inclined to be philosophical. A husband likes to be praised by his wife and if he does not find recognition at home, he seeks it elsewhere. Though he enjoys the praise of others and occasionally likes to brag, usually he does not gloat. When working on a project, that "project" may become more important to him than issues concerning his wife and children. This work may engulf him and become his entire world. Achieving success in this given sphere becomes his main priority. During such times, a wife who feels abandoned by her husband and has made unsuccessful attempts to draw her husband's attention, may establish a relationship with a man who is willing to spend time with her. An initially innocent friendship may eventually lead to a romantic attachment, which in turn may cause her to leave her husband.

A wife should remember that men do not like to be "mothered." Fundamentally, a husband should be - more so than a wife – emotionally balanced. He also has an inner need to protect his wife and children. He, a man, reacts quickly to outside sexual stimulation. When hurt, he is able to withstand the difficult and humiliating times of helplessness; he does not "fall into pieces" as his wife may.

It is not enough to ask, who is a man and a woman in their marriage, but rather, who should they be? The answers depend on their point of view. These various viewpoints influence the differing and even opposing opinions. Examining one's thoughts on this fundamental question, however, tends to "refresh" a marriage.

Traits a husband and a wife should have

The man, as the husband in the sacramental marriage, should care for and love his wife, have time to talk with her, be gentle, sensitive, hard-working, well-behaved and sober in his thinking. To the best of his ability, he should be educated and ready to take up his role, be responsible for his words and actions, reasonable, consequential, prudent, cultural and neat in his appearance. He should keep peace and order in the home, be self-controlled and welcoming of guests. He should be without addictions (smoking, drinking, gambling, television or computer). He should not be an egotist, a dictator or a materialist. He should have a good reputation and be straightforward. Finally, he should always be guided by the principles of the Catholic faith, and not just pretend to be a Catholic to make a good impression during the engagement and to be married in the Church.

The woman, as the wife in a sacramental marriage, should above all, love her husband. She should be caring, devoted, warm, worthy of respect and trust, appreciative of her husband, educated, gentle and prudent. She should not be egotistical or a gossip. She should know the value of silence and be elegant in her dress. She should be without addictions (smoking, drinking, gambling, gossiping, television programs, talking on the phone). She should be a good hostess, as well as be economical and thrifty in managing household expenses. She should maintain a clean and organized home. Finally, she should always be guided by the principles of her Catholic faith.

These are beautiful traits, but where would you find such a husband or a wife? Being too picky and fickle while searching for an ideal spouse could leave you an old maid or an old bachelor. This does not mean you should give up searching for the best candidate for a husband or wife. This person will surely not be easy to find, however, it is worth the trouble to find the right one. Look for someone who not only has a beautiful figure and noteworthy intellect, but more importantly, someone who has a wonderfully balanced spirituality, a loving heart and possesses wisdom (do not confuse this with knowledge).

God created man and woman. He gave them the gifts they needed to be able to realize their natural vocation (fatherhood and motherhood – physical and spiritual), their life roles (such as their careers), as well as, the ultimate goal of their lives (salvation). Not every couple, however, enjoys the privilege of having their own biological children. Married couples can adopt children to form a family. Without children, however, they can still experience their sacramental vocation to marriage in a wonderful way, being sanctified with God's help to reach heaven as the ultimate goal in their lives Remember, however, it is a child that most enriches the relationship of the married couple and their vocation to fatherhood and motherhood.

5. Who Should a Father and Mother be?

A married couple should understand that the gift to give life comes from God. John Paul II in his *Letter to the Family* writes: "Human fatherhood and motherhood, while remaining biologically similar to that of other living beings in nature, contain in an essential and unique way a 'likeness' to God, which is the basis of the family as a community of human life, as a community of persons united in love *(communio personarum)*." (nr. 6)

"In particular, responsible fatherhood and motherhood directly concern the moment in which a man and a woman, uniting themselves 'in one flesh', can become parents. This is a moment of special value both for their interpersonal relationship and for their service to life: they can become parents – father and mother – by communicating life to a new human being. *The two dimensions of conjugal union*, the unitive and the procreative, *cannot be artificially separated* without damaging the deepest truth of the conjugal act itself." (nr. 12)

"...the conjugal union, the biblical '*una caro*', can be understood and fully explained *only by recourse to the values of the 'person' and of 'gift'*. Every man and every woman fully realizes himself or herself through the sincere gift of self. For spouses, the moment of conjugal union constitutes a very particular expression of this. Then a man and woman, in the 'truth' of their masculinity and femininity, become a mutual gift to each other." (nr. 12)

"In the conjugal act, husband and wife are called to confirm in a responsible way *the mutual gift* of self which they have made to each other in the marriage covenant. The logic of the *total gift of self to the other* involves a potential openness to procreation: in this way the marriage is called to even greater fulfillment as a family. Certainly the mutual gift of husband and wife does not have the begetting of children as its only end, but is in itself a mutual communion of love and of life." (nr 12)

Relationships within a family are much more enriching and responsible than in a marriage. The main role of the couple continues to be their mutual help in attaining the ultimate goal of holiness and salvation. The parent's duty is not only to receive children and raise them as Catholics, but also to encompass them with their parental love and to help them one day to be able to say, with gratitude, "I BELIEVE AND LOVE GOD! Thank you for the beautiful gifts of life, faith and the love of God and people!"

I wish for you, with all my priestly heart, that someday, when your children are adults, you will experience such a wonderful moment.

6. The Essential Stages of Human Development

- **Prenatal stage** – this is the most dynamic period of human development which takes place in the mother's womb during the blessed state of pregnancy. This is a time where great care should be taken for the health of the mother and child; a time to pray for the baby and a time for the mother to pray with the baby in her womb (especially from the first moments of the new life of the child who absorbs all of the mother's reactions);
- **Infant to preschool stage** – this incredibly important time is when the main blueprint of person's life is developed (from birth to 5 years), this period in the child's life requires the particular presence of the mother, who in

being at home with the child, constantly reassures the child's feeling of being loved and safe;

- **School age stage** (from 6 years old to pre-adolescence) – this is a time for development at home and at school; a time of being influenced by parents and other adult role models, a time for catechism and the beginning of sacramental life, a time for girls to play with dolls and younger children (first signs of motherhood), a time to demonstrating affection naturally, to increase modesty in the children's dress and their limited awareness of their sexuality. This is a time to teach them to be wary of strangers (to protect them from sexual abuse). It is also a time for discipline, especially boys;

- **Preadolescent stage** – this is the first period of youth, a stage when feelings of love and the sexual drive awaken, a time of making or avoiding contact with others, a time to discover the joys of life, a time of being shy of strangers and a time for first encounters with failure. This is a stage where parents are very sensitive to the physical and psychological changes in their children and when parents should begin, with respect and sensitivity, to teach their children about their sexuality, to help them accept their sex, purity and modesty (daughters may be taught about their fertility cycles and sons should learn about their psychological and emotional development). It is also a time to teach them about the need to follow their conscience according to God's plan.

The moral formation of children and the development of their conscience are necessary, but must be supported with the knowledge of the moral teachings of the Catholic Church. The main reference for helping couples and parents deepen their knowledge is the "compact" version of the *Catechism of the Catholic Church* (the *Compendium*).

"Moral conscience, present at the heart of the person, enjoins him at the appropriate moment to do good and avoid evil. It also judges particular choices, approving those that are good and denouncing those that are evil. It bears witness to the authority of truth in reference to the supreme Good to which the human person is drawn, and it welcomes the commandments. When he listens to his conscience, the prudent man can hear God speaking."
(nr. 1777)

"Conscience is a judgment of reason whereby the human person recognizes the moral quality of a concrete act that he is going to perform is in the process of performing, or has already completed. In all he says and does, man is obliged to follow faithfully what he knows to be just and right." (nr. 1778)

"The dignity of the human person implies and requires uprightness of moral conscience. Conscience includes the perception of the principles of morality (synderesis); their application in the given circumstances by practical discernment of reasons and goods; and finally judgment about concrete acts yet to be preformed or already performed." (nr. 1780)

"Conscience enables one to assume responsibility for the acts preformed....In attesting to the fault committed, it calls to mind the forgiveness that must be asked..." (nr. 1781)

"Man has the right to act in conscience and in freedom so as personally to make moral decisions. 'He must not be forced to act contrary to his conscience...'" (nr. 1782)

It can be said that the conscience is "god within us" or Christ's inner voice, which calls us to follow Him.

- **Youth** – this is a time to plan your life and find your vocation with the help of your parents (as well as discovering and realizing it), a time to uncover the gifts that God has given you (the role of parents and their personal experiences are irreplaceable since young people search for positive role models at this time) and a time of problems with chastity (masturbation, which can become an addiction with boys, can lead them toward experimentation with homosexuality, while it can lead girls to lose their virginity and lesbian experimentation, leaving behind painful memories and emotions). This is also a time for serious discussions with parents, who should explain that experimenting with sex will destroy the ability to love a person of the opposite sex, will lead to sexual egoism, and in the future, to the rejection of the possibility of becoming mothers or fathers (egoism in the couple is the beginning of a mentality that accepts anti-conception and abortion. This is a time for open and honest, though difficult, dialog between children and their parents;

- **Maturity** - this is a time to choose your path in life (marriage or celibacy, including religious or priestly life) and make responsible choices, which may include accompanying or providing assistance to parents or other specific forms of help.

It takes a lot of time and money to educate your children. Knowledge, however, is only the intellectual "part" of a person. Intellectual formation, although not the most important, is necessary to help the will of a person to make appropriate and responsible decisions. Religious formation should not be neglected during a person's intellectual formation, as it provides the necessary motivation to do good and reject evil. A person should consult with God when making decisions and take direction from the official (!) teachings of the Catholic Church. Otherwise, he may use the knowledge against himself, others and God.

Not every child has highly intellectually abilities. Parents should help less talented children, motivate them and praise even their smallest successes in their education. The talented ones, on the other hand, should have their pride curbed so that they do not become arrogant. Talents are gifts. It is important to measure a child's efforts, not just results. This is the way it should be in a family, since the rest of the world measures only success. A child needs to be prepared for this difference as well. A human being should be valued for being a human being.

The more important is the formation of a child's heart, spirituality and ability to love. Ultimately, the most important decisions are made within one's heart. Spiritual formation must develop the ability to love. It is not enough to have knowledge of moral values; but rather, a more personal example of elders in the family – starting with the father and mother – is essential. Without this type of example, even true words about love will sound false. A Latin proverb says, "words instruct, examples lead." Many children are more expensive to raise, but easier to bring up (the oldest child needs to be particularly well-raised, since he will be an example for the younger siblings!) In raising children, there should be a balance between mind and heart. Engaged and newly married couples (at the beginning) should find this balance for themselves if they have not already done so.

In the book, *Psychology of Human Development - Characteristics of the Phases of Human Life* (Volume 2, Barbara Harwas-Napierala and Janusz Trempala, Warsaw, 2000), we find the following phases of human development:

- **prenatal period:** from conception to birth
- **childhood:**
  - early (from birth to 3 years of age)
  - middle (from 4 years of age)
  - later (from 7 years of age)
- **adolescence:**
  - early (from 10/12 years of age)
  - later (from 14/16 years of age)
- **adulthood:**
  - early (from 20/23 years of age)
  - middle (from 35/40 years of age)
  - later (from 55/60 years of age)

I would like to note that psychologists are not in agreement as to the number of phases and their division by age. It is also possible to write more detail about each of these stages of human development. Since this book is religious in nature, I undertook a different approach to this topic. The richness of the human life is endless and it is probably not possible to describe it in an exhaustive manner.

There are many different kinds of people and each individual is a miracle of God and humanity.

7. Being Raised to Love

Raising children to love should encompass the following truths and principles of behavior:

1. Love and sexuality, God's holy gifts to humanity, are the best language of communication with Him and another person.
2. At the end of life, only love remains, and we will have to give an account of our love; even the great gifts of faith and hope will pass.
3. A person needs love for his full development on earth, and after his biological death, for his eternal life with God.
4. Teaching about love should always be connected to God and His teachings (commandments) as proclaimed by the Catholic Church; otherwise, it will be false.
5. There are many stages of love in a person's life, which depend on the degree of the individual's development and inner disposition; remember, the first stage of love is "not to do evil" to the person you love!
6. Every evil (sin) diminishes the ability to love and can even lead to the acceptance of evil as good (satanic inversion, and spitefulness).
7. Human love requires sacrifice: the greatest was given by Jesus Christ, Son of God, who became Man and in His

love for us, died on the cross, so that we could truly love God and others.

8. The liberal media and education in schools often insidiously secularize the gift of love, by separating it from God, making it perversely erotic, lying about it, deforming it, propagating forms of deviation as normal and manipulating the hearts of people who long for authentic love - hearts created by God for true love (education about Catholic moral teaching is necessary).

9. Children and youth need to be introduced and taught gradually about the sexual and the erotic dimensions of human love, but not by being presented with any erotic materials, because they falsify the true meaning of love, presenting the physical aspect as its most important value, whereby in reality, it is only an exterior form of the interior value that is love. Tasteless, insinuating and vulgar jokes are unacceptable.

10. Children should be taught from the beginning about chastity and respect for sexuality, as well as, their roles and goal within God's plan.

11. It is necessary to oppose those who falsify the truth about love and sexuality, because they erode the delicate and pure hearts of children.

12. Parents should obtain appropriate knowledge of Catholic sexual ethics and be the first ones to teach their children about love and sexuality, preferably, individually and with sons and daughters separately. Parents can also allow someone trustworthy and with the appropriate knowledge to teach their children about Catholic morals, including sexual ethics.

13. Parents should ask their pastors to hold meetings in their parish that will help them learn about Catholic ethics and morality.

It is worthwhile to gather Catholic knowledge in these areas now, since various responsibilities will take up your precious time later. Putting off your children's questions about sexuality with words like: "leave me alone," "I don't have time right now," "go to your mother (or father)," and so on, is a tremendous parenting error. This type of treatment will decrease a child's openness, make them feel uneasy and although it may divert their attention for awhile, their curious minds will only be more determined to discover the answers. When going to others or strangers to find the answers, children may receive them in a brutal and vulgar form, which will shock their young minds and write itself deep within their memories and emotions, distorting their hearts. Then a very serious and painful parenting problem will emerge that will be difficult to rectify.

Parents should have Catholic literature for themselves as well as their children that are at the appropriate emotional and intellectual level of the child. Parents also need to be aware of their children's Internet use and should protect them from sites that vulgarize sex and the sexuality of men and women, as well as propagate liberal moral values. I want to draw attention to school programs, even in Catholic schools. As parents, you are the first in line who is responsible before God for your children's upbringing, not their teachers, priests or catechists. Be ready to come to the aid of your children at the right time. Do not allow your children be harmed in the name of the false "love" propagated by schools or the media (newspapers, radio, TV, movies, music). This damage will be difficult to repair. The child will become distrustful of even his own parents. They will resent you for not protecting them from these deprivations.

A Moment of Reflection and Dialog

1. First, individually write down all your positive and negative qualities, then look at them together and see if these qualities will help you build a marital relationship.

2. Talk about whether or not each of you wants to further develop yourselves as human beings (intellectually, psychologically, culturally, religiously and emotionally) and what kind of help you need.

3. Think about how you can help one another in furthering your personal development.

III. Being a Person of Dialog

1. The Basic Forms of Dialog

- with yourself, your innermost being (the first and most necessary communication);
- with others, in order to be part of a community of people ("no man is an island");
- with God – the Father, Son and the Holy Spirit, to be in communion with Him (the most important relationship).

In Ancient Greece, in Delphi, there was a "strange" temple. People would go inside to discover their innermost being. At the entrance to the temple a sign said in Greek: *gnoti se auton* - "know thyself."

In the Gospel, Christ talked about the body as a temple, and St. Paul reminded Christians that they are a temple in which God lives.

We do not have to travel to the temple in Delphi to contemplate our innermost being and get to know ourselves better. Every one of us, in the quiet of our inner being, can and should find themselves. You should find the time for yourself and teach yourself how to communicate with your innermost being. This most intimate dialog with yourself is crucial. Without this dialog, it is difficult, if not impossible, to communicate properly with others. Yet, the basis for both of these dialogs is your dialog with God, realized through prayer. Only God can teach us how to communicate with love and respect – with ourselves and others.

Our dialog with God should never be forced or considered a duty or a waste of time. This dialog with God is always a benefit to the person, the people in his community, and especially his spouse.

Marriage should be the safest place for communication, since the dialog takes place between two people who love each other as husband and wife. They should be the two people who know each other best and love each other most of all. Every dialog between them should be born from love and truth. Marital dialog comes from two hearts united in everyday love. True communication requires the open hearts and minds of both spouses in dealing with marriage and family matters.

This communication is inherent in the dialog of a person with himself and others, and most importantly with God. A person of prayer is a person of dialog.

2. Communication during Engagement and Marriage

- You have to prepare for dialog, especially when there are difficult issues to discuss (pray and search within yourself for positive solutions).
- Dialog is necessary in every engagement and marriage.
  A dialog is not a monologue; it does not consist only of words (about 30%), but also gestures and body language. Pay attention to words that refer to important topics (their logic and validity), your body's reaction during the dialog (peaceful or explosive), and remember to consider your husband's or wife's point of view.
- The words that you chose for your discussions need to be very clear to both parties, therefore you should avoid being unclear (misunderstood words should be clarified at once).
- Honesty, openness and effort to seek the common good is necessary.
- When discussing positive and negative traits, you should not praise yourself, while destroying your fiancé or spouse with criticism (the time and place of dialog is not a trial and court room).

- It is important to have a positive attitude toward your fiancé or spouse before and during your dialog (negative emotions should be set aside, as you concentrate on the essence of the matter being discussed).
- The dialog should be based on the truth (facts), a clearly presented point of view and a search for a mutual solution.
- It is not acceptable to manipulate a person, take advantage of their lack of knowledge or "play" with his or her emotions (especially those of a woman, a wife).
- Remember the risk of having someone take advantage of your trust and using you; it is good to slowly and wisely "uncover your cards."
- Concentrate on the issue at hand and do not suppress your feelings regarding the problem being discussed.
- Respect one another and do not ridicule the other person's shortcomings.
- Specific times should be set for (monthly) meetings and a system of rules for discussion established (however, in certain situations, immediate attention is required).
- Both sides should work on implementing the agreed upon solutions and, after a time, discuss their realization.
- Prayer should begin and complete your dialog (prayers should be said out loud, but can also be said in silence – especially after a difficult discussion).

"Silent days" should encourage a meeting and marital dialog; time alone will not unravel difficult issues or automatically heal pain.

3. Conflicts during Engagement and Marriage
a) Sources of conflict:

1. Decisions involving a major change made by one of the parties without the consent of the other.

2. Inappropriate behavior: excessive attention to oneself, overly excessive demands, coldness and indifference, avoiding contact, hostility, bickering, being together due to necessity.

3. Sexual problems (during marriage): giving in to relentless demands of the other person, greater sexual drive of one side, using sex to resolve problems, egotistical sex, difficult living arrangements, lack of understanding of the different needs of women and men, temporary difficulties (unemployment, sickness, financial problems), forcing sex (usually by the man) when there is a lack of loving atmosphere throughout the day.

4. Humiliating the fiancé or spouse in front of others (family, friends or acquaintances).

5. Frequently putting the opinion of others above those of your fiancé or spouse.

6. Feeling constantly dependant on the other person (for example: "he always has to be right, always controls the money, while I have to walk on eggshells so that there is peace in the house").

It is important to remember that there are also benefits to conflicts during you engagement and marriage. They give you a chance to learn about yourself and your spouse; they help in your personal development and when properly addressed, they deepen your love for one another. During conflicts, you may need the help of a third party, who is prepared and experienced. This could be a psychologist or a sexologist (especially if they are also practicing Catholics), or a priest who provides counseling to married couples. Their presence makes it easier to hear each other's point of view and find positive solutions to the conflict.

The following occurred in Silver Springs, Maryland, not far from Washington, D.C., in the United States. An American woman of Polish decent came to the parish office one day and asked for help, because, as she said, no American priest would help her. She explained the problems she and her husband were having and that he had already filed for divorce in court. With her permission, I took notes as she spoke, hoping that they would be useful when I met with her husband, who would explain his side of the story. We arranged for them to come in together at a given time. First, she talked about the problems. We both listened. Then it was his turn. Here, we were taken by surprise. Instead of giving us "his version", he said: "Father, I will withdraw the divorce petition from the court." Afterwards, I received a thank you letter from her. That had been our second and final meeting. I never saw them again. I do not know if they are together or not, but from time to time I pray for them. This is why sometimes a third person is needed, so that both people can hear each other.

During my meetings with married couples who were experiencing difficulties, I often noticed that it was more difficult for the men to speak, especially in the presence of their wives and a priest, and even more so when they had to admit to being at fault. Husbands often ignore problems and say they are no big deal. I hear about most cases involving marital problems from wives first. It is they who want to save the family or the marriage. The wives looked for help, since their prayers and persuasion were not enough. I could not ignore the cold behavior of the husbands and the justified pain of the wives; these issues should have been addressed immediately. Very often, the threat of divorce existed, because the wife had simply had enough of this kind of life. In such cases I was forced to tell the husbands painful but truthful words about their problems and they way they ignored their wives. Thank goodness, God helped us in these situations. Together, we found solutions for the good of the marriage and family. In every case, we were able to avoid divorce or separation, which would have been a tragedy for the marriage and the family (when children were involved). Both sides, at a certain moment, wanted to continue their lives together. For these successes, we thanked God together in prayer, and later, I myself, in the chapel, thanked Jesus and Mary for their help!

b) Conflict Resolution Methods

1. Both sides have to admit there is a problem or conflict.
2. Both sides have to have good intentions and want to talk.
3. First, find the right time and a peaceful place.
4. At the beginning, ask the Holy Spirit for help.
5. Remember that a man accepts arguments in a rational way, while his wife (as the more emotional of the two) needs to be heard, comforted and helped in a specific way.
6. After both sides calm their emotions, then find the time to talk and listen (do not interrupt when the other person is talking).
7. Always look for positive solutions together and for your mutual good.
8. Do not favor yourself or hide your faults (call it as it is).
9. See the good in each other (everyone has some good traits).
10. Together, search for solution to future problems (after removing the main causes of the conflict).
11. Both sides must make a decision and put it into practice together (from time to time, checking the progress of the mutual decision).
12. Before ending the discussion, forgive each other and ask God for forgiveness – if the conflict was serious, both of you should go to confession (close the past and do not return to it – this is very important!!!!).
13. End the dialog by praying together.
14. After the discussion, find a way to relax together (for example, go out for coffee or take a walk).

A Moment of Reflection and Dialog

1. Talk about who you keep in touch with (prepare lists of people with explanations and then go over it together).
2. Discuss who you would like to stay in touch with and why.
3. Make another list of people with whom you should keep in touch (family, friends and others).
4. Decide how you will establish new relationships and **cut off ties with the people who separate you from your spouse, even if they are close to your heart!** Try to connect with people who believe in God and are positive.

IV. Being a Sexual Person

1. God's Plan for your Gender

God the Creator gave people the gift of different genders, and through this gift, He gave each person a corresponding role. A person, through his or her gender, longs to enter into intimate relationships: to give himself or herself as a gift and receive the other person as a gift. Original sin caused disharmony in humans. The sin of disobedience brought about "interior disorder" - a tendency to do the evil that is forbidden. For the first time, the human experienced disharmony and shame when he noticed his nakedness and tried to cover it up. Before, there was no problem with it. Christ, stripped and dying on the cross, returned to man the priority of spirit over flesh. In the Sacrament of Marriage, Jesus sanctifies every action of the married couple, including their sexual acts which are open to giving new human life.

Jesus did not negate the gift of a person's sexuality, but made it holy, so that mutual and fertile love of a married couple could develop. Sexuality cannot be guided by instinct or biology. A person is responsible for the gift of sexuality. Standing guard of this gift is the sixth commandment, "do not commit adultery", which was given to the chosen people and all humanity at Sinai when God established the covenant. In the Gospel, Christ incessantly reminds us of the value of this commandment.

The complete giving of yourself to your spouse and the acceptance of your spouse's gift to you – through the intimate sexual union – should always be open to new life within the Sacrament of Marriage. The Sacrament sanctifies every aspect of married life, including sexual acts. They are written into God's eternal plan and through these acts, the married couple realizes it. God gifted sexuality to humans and requires us to use it responsibly.

Married couples should make themselves familiar with the functioning of female and male sexuality. Engaged couples needs to become familiar with the Natural Family Planning method, not to use it as a method of anti-conception and to avoid having children, but rather as a way to be able to choose the right time to have children.

Human sexuality requires mutual sensitivity and respect of the husband and wife. This gift should be enjoyed with complete love and freedom. Otherwise, it may cause pain and lead to withdrawal, to searching for intimacy beyond the marriage (infidelity of the spirit and body), to suspicions and unhappiness, and even to tragedy or divorce. Sexual abuse during marriage leaves deep wounds and destroys affectionate married love. Among young married couples, 80 percent list sexual dissatisfaction as a reason for an unhappy marriage.

Sexual intercourse enhances the experience of femininity and masculinity, strengthens the marital bond and intensifies the feelings and love between spouses. It should never be an act of egoism by one or both persons. It should take into consideration the sexual needs, feelings, psychological and spiritual needs of both spouses. Sex should never be "the use" of another person's body to satisfy one's own pleasures (as a form of "free prostitution" within marriage). A healthy sexual life in marriage, based on respect and love, helps keep the marriage strong and faithful, while preventing infidelity.

Sexual Shame

This is the unpleasant feeling that results when a person and his intimate being are treated as an object, degrading his personal dignity and self worth. The feeling of shame reveals the connection between a person's moral and natural orders. There exists a spontaneous need to conceal a person's sexual values. This sexual shame protects the dignity and self worth of a person as a human being.

"Sexual modesty is not a flight from love, but on the contrary the opening of a way towards it. *The spontaneous need to conceal mere sexual values bound up with the person is the natural way to the discovery of the value of the person as such.* The value of the person is closely connected with its inviolability, its status as 'something more than an object of use'. Sexual modesty is as it were a defensive reflex, which protects that status and so protects the value of the person (...). To say that shame is 'absorbed' by love does not mean that it is eliminated or destroyed. Quite the contrary – it is reinforced, in man and woman, for only where it is preserved intact can love be realized in full. 'Absorption' means only that love fully utilizes for its own purposes the characteristic effects of shame, and specifically that awareness of the proper relationship between the value of the person and sexual values which shame introduces as a natural and spontaneous feeling into the mutual relationship of man and woman (...). The law of the absorption of shame by love helps us to understand the whole problem of chastity or rather of conjugal modesty at the level of psychology. (...) only true love, a love which possesses in full the ethical essence proper to it, is capable of absorbing shame" (K. Wojtyla, *Love and Responsibility*, Ignatius Press, San Francisco, 1993, p.p. 179-183).

"Sexual shame – is simply treating a person's body, according to their gender, in a way that the person deserves. We come to know a person through his body; he allows us to learn about him through his body; and to whom we express reverence, respect and love through the intercession of his body. Shame is, therefore, an expression of respect to oneself and others" (K. Meissner, B. Suszka, *Your Future*, Poznan 2001, p.53).

Modesty is often an effective deterrent and protection against being taken advantage of for an opportunity to have sex outside of marriage. It is worth mentioning the attire of girls and women at this point. Their clothing should be appropriate. "Showing too much skin" lowers the value of a woman and, in the eyes of boys and men, makes her into an object of lust and the butt of lewd jokes. A person's dress can send a message about who that person is. Even though it is said that "clothes don't make a person", they are still an exterior indication of how the person views his or her own self worth. A women's clothing can account for whether or not she is respected. Unaware of the effects of wearing inappropriate clothing, a girl or a woman may acquire a bad reputation or even become a victim of rape.

"What is truly immodest in dress is that which frankly contributes to the deliberate displacement of the true value of the person by sexual values, that which is bound to elicit a reaction to the person as to 'a possible means of obtaining sexual enjoyment' and not 'a possible object of love by reason of his or her personal value'" (K. Wojtyla, *Love and Responsibility*, p.190).

I remember when the girls and women in Rome would borrow shawls or scarves to cover their bare shoulders and the upper parts of their bodies when passing by the guards at the doors of St. Peter's Basilica to enter. St. Paul taught women to cover their heads in church. When I came first to America, I saw women with scarves covering their heads during Holy Mass, but now this custom has almost disappeared.

Nudism falsely propagates the public mingling of both sexes while in the nude as a form of freedom that regenerates one's physical and psychological health. Nudity in itself is not negative; however, its public display can lead to immoral provocation and behavior (nude séances, lewd and sexual thoughts and unethical sexual behaviors, and so on). God the Creator created people in His own likeness and image. The human being was a completely good and noble creation. *The man and the woman were both naked, yet they felt no shame* (Gn 2:25). It was only after the sin of disobedience that man and woman, for the first time, experienced their nakedness painfully: they covered themselves and ran away from God: *"Then the eyes of both of them were opened, and they knew they were naked; so they sewed fig leaves together and made* *loincloths for themselves. When they heard the sound of the Lord God walking about in the garden... the man and his wife hid themselves from the Lord God among the trees... The Lord God then called to the man and asked him: Where are you? He answered, "I heard you in the garden; but I was afraid, because I was naked, so I hid."* (Gn 3: 7-11). Nudism is a sin against God and the human person, because it scandalizes, impoverishes the relationship between a man and woman, encourages "taking advantage" of the occasion, dulls a person emotionally and sexually, and may deprive him of the desire to marry (A. Marcol, *Ethics of Sexual Life*, Opole 1998, p.84).

Chastity

Chastity not only protects human sexuality and dignity, but also ensures that the spirit prevails over the flesh and sensual lust. It also helps a married couple to enjoy their sexual life in accordance with God's plan. Chastity is needed not only during the engagement period, but during marriage as well! Chastity in marriage includes: love, faithfulness, honesty, unity, and marital sex that is open to giving life.

"Love One Another," is one of the most popular Catholic magazines in Poland, dedicating many of its pages to young people and married couples. It is published in seven languages (Polish, Russian, English, Slovak, Hungarian, Romanian and even Ethiopian). The magazine established the Movement of Pure Hearts (MPH) and the Movement of Pure Married Hearts (MPMH). These movements came into being in answer to Pope John Paul II's call to support and save family values - the "little Church." The testimony of those who joined MPH and MPMH is filled with joy and gratitude to God for all wonderful graces that they received by joining the movement, promoting the purity of heart as a special value in the lives of young people searching their own path and shape for their love, as well as, in their married lives.

Principles of the MPMH Movement

1. Most importantly, spouses promise to pray every day and offer themselves and their children to Jesus, who is the source of married love, and to strengthen their love to God in the Trinity.
2. Live always in a state of grace, and in case of mortal sin, to seek out confession as quickly as possible.
3. Recognize God's plan; work together with Him and to accept any children He wishes to give.
4. After receiving Holy Communion, recite this prayer of offering:

"I offer to you O Lord, myself, my memory, my mind, my soul and my body. Teach me to love my wife (husband) and children, who come from you. Jesus Christ, give us both hearts that are pure like Your own, so that our union will form our love to be wise, generous, committed, unselfish and a guardian of Your laws and commandments. May daily family prayer, the rosary and the chaplet of Divine Mercy, attending Holy Mass together and receiving the Holy Communion help us; may every serious fall be immediately confessed in the sacrament of confession. Allow us to always draw from the graces of the sacrament of marriage.

Lord Jesus, be the only Lord of our lives. Teach me to acquire the ability to control my sexual impulses and emotions, so that the love I have for my wife (husband) and children, will not depend upon my moods and emotional states, but rather on my constant care and never ending affirmation of what is good. I ask you for pure marital love, that I may be a pure and unselfish gift to my spouse. Purify our love from all egoism, so that we are always able to forgive each other, without hiding resentment, and pray for one another.

In order to preserve my purity, I resolve not to read, buy or look at any magazines, programs or films of a pornographic nature. I will not to use any forms of anti-conception and will be ready to accept every child that God bestows upon us.

I ask you, Lord, for help in avoiding everything that causes addiction, enslaves or encourages evil. Mary, my Mother, lead me along the path of faith to the source of love in our marriage – so that I can always trust and believe in Him. Amen."

The Movement of Pure Hearts (MPH)

Anyone who will fulfill the commitments of the Movement of Pure Hearts may become a member. They are found in this Prayer of Offering:

"Lord Jesus, thank you for loving me with a grace that lifts me up from my greatest falls and heals my most painful wounds.

I give to you, my Lord, my memory, my mind, my will, my soul and body, as well as, my sexuality. I promise not to engage in sexual activity until I enter into the Sacrament of Marriage. I promise not to buy, read, or look at magazines, programs or films that are pornographic in nature. (Girls may add: I promise to dress modestly and in no way provoke lustful thoughts or desires in others.).

I promise to meet with You in daily prayer, when reading the Holy Bible, frequently receiving the Holy Communion and in the Adoration of the Holy Sacrament. I resolve to receive the Sacrament of Reconciliation regularly, not to give in to discouragement and to rise quickly from my sins. Lord Jesus, teach me to work systematically on improving myself, teach me how to control my sexual impulses and emotions.

Please give me courage in my struggle against peer pressure, so that I may never take drugs and that I may avoid everything that causes addiction, especially alcohol and nicotine.

Teach me to behave in such a way, so that the most important thing in my life is Love.

Mary, my Mother, lead me in ways of faith to the very source of love, to Jesus. With the God's Servant, John Paul II, I want to offer myself to you: 'Totus Tuus (*Tota Tua*), Mary!' Into your Immaculate Heart, I offer my whole being, everything that I am, my every step, every moment of my life. Blessed Caroline, intercede on my behalf, in asking for the gift of a pure heart. Amen!"

Virginity

Virginity, celibacy and the sublimation of the sex drive does not destroy a person, nor does it limit his full development, but rather, it becomes a conscious, loving gift offered to God or one's future spouse. Many prominent people, for the sake of success in their fields, or due to necessity, give up marital sexual relations for a time (athletes, scholars, sailors, travelers, people working on overseas assignments, long term migrants), until they are reunited with their wives and families again. In the history of the Church, there have been couples and parents that have given up sex for a period of time or all together (for example, St. Lucy), even for life, as a gift to God. Of course, if this sacrifice is temporary and necessary, then it has a justified earthy value. However, if the sacrifice is enduring and offered as a gift to God, then its value deserved to be recognized by others and surely by God.

The Function of Gender

Your sex distinguishes you as male or female. This gift of gender is the foundation of the intimate unity of body and soul between spouses, through which, with the help of God, a new person is called into being.

Your gender has certain specific functions:
* creates life within marriage,

- is a form of communication between spouses,
- offers erotic and sensual pleasure,
- ensures the existence of the human race,
- liberates and makes spouses more sensitive to one another,
- gives the opportunity to be responsible for life within your marriage.

Your gender helps create lifelong connections. The experience of these connections is directed toward the possibility of creating a new person: a child, who as a person is the external and permanent fruit of the intimate union of husband and wife. The different characteristics of the opposite sexes complement, rather than exclude, each other. Experiencing your sexuality helps engaged couples (without having sexual intercourse) and married couples (including sexual intercourse) in their personal development.

Sexual Ethics

Married couple received their ethical norms from God. The Church interprets God's Revelation and reminds people about them. Sexual intercourse between spouses should be based on Catholic moral teaching and Revelation. During sexual intercourse, spouses are persons; they are not objects "to be used." Catholic moral principles help spouses to develop true sexual marital love, endure difficult situations in their sexual love (misunderstandings, sexual incompetence, permanent handicaps and prolonged separation) and avoid seeking out "erotic adventure" outside of marriage. Marital intercourse requires sexual refinement, responsible parenting and incorporating the Natural Family Planning method. Abuse develops egoism and selfishness, which leads to the disappearance of love, Catholic morals and sensitivity toward one's spouse. Sex, when "used" during youth and the engagement (by about 75%) and deprived of these ethical values, negatively affects marital life and very often leads to divorce (about 90%).

Natural Family Planning (NFP)

These methods are in line with God's plan and are not harmful. They take advantage of a woman's natural cycle of fertility and infertility. These methods require abstinence from sexual intercourse during a woman's fertile time, waiting and taking advantage of days that are infertile, if the married couple, for some reason, wishes to avoid conception for a time. During fertile times, however, the couple can be conscious and fairly confident that their sexual union will bring about new life – a new person. The known methods are: the Ogino-Knaus method (the oldest, "calendar method" which is effective, with regular cycles, about 90% of the time; with irregular cycles, about 53%); the Creighton method (up to 99.3% effective according to the research of Frank-Herm); the Billings Ovulation method from Australia (up to 98% effective) and the Sympto-thermal (up to 99.8% effective according to the research of Joseph Rotzer). It is necessary to become familiar with these methods to effectively employ them. *These methods are more accurate than anti-conception methods and do not have harmful side effects!* Natural methods also give you a peaceful conscience, joy during intercourse and the psychological luxury of not worrying about pregnancy. These methods allow both spouses to be treated with respect (neither is "taken advantage of" nor "used"), they do not destroy fertility, protect the couple from falling into a routine, help husbands be more sensitive toward their wives, and deepen the spouse's love for each other. Furthermore, it costs nothing. Engaged couples should research these methods, so that later as married couples they can use them to plan for their desired children. Married couples who use NFP can be experienced and authoritative teachers for their adult children who are preparing for marriage. Naturally, the liberal media will omit the authenticity and effectiveness of these natural methods as well as their harmlessness (anti-conception and abortion is a very lucrative business). Furthermore, the planned secularization of society and the fight against the Catholic Church supported by liberal political parties, justify positions that are not moral norms, and for through reasons known to them aim at decreasing the natural growth of certain populations. Natural Family Planning strengthens the marital bond and help couples get through various crises (only about 1.5% of marriages using Natural Planning Methods end in divorce).

"Through the end of the last century, anti-life propaganda did not subside. Supporters of killing babies in their mothers' wombs, using abortive methods and anti-conception, branded those propagating Natural Family Planning as 'ignorant, backward and stuck in the Middle Ages.' They tried to insinuate to society that the natural regulation of conception is an invention of the 'uneducated women of the Church.' These hostile verbal attacks were used with a specific goal in mind. It could be, for example, a battle over public opinion, an effort to market anti-conception product, loosening of public morality, or an effort to hide their ignorance. If we tested their knowledge about the physiology of fertility and the basic methods of recognizing it, the loudest critics of Natural Family Planning would not have much to say. The lack of knowledge about Natural Family Planning is what is 'ignorant and backward'! These critics question scientific research and try to discredit credible, effective and ecological methods of understanding human fertility. The fear of NFP in certain communities seems to be rationalized with the knowledge that modern methods of recognized fertility naturally may lead to the disappearance of artificial methods that interfere with the cycle. Who would want to buy products that are harmful (physically, psychologically and spiritually) to prevent fertility, if they could independently recognize their own natural rhythm of fertility? The comments of certain NFP critics give the impression that it is easier to persuade others that they are uneducated and backward, than to admit their own incompetence in the matter.

"In 1966, the World Health Organization put out a report confirming the effectiveness of Natural Family Planning.

In 1993, WHO presented a document entitled Family Planning and Population Division of Family Health. This document contains recommendations that refer to: the promotion of methods to recognize fertility, the organization of conferences on this subject, preparing informational materials and programs that teach specific methods, training for people teaching these methods, translation of literature on the recognition of fertility, financing of counseling in this area, including the teaching of fertility recognition in all health programs provided for children and adults, the assistance of fertility experts to help develop and implement programs, preparing instructional materials for men, education workers in basic health care in this area, a call to all European countries to create a multidisciplinary team to promote and educate in the area of fertility recognition. WHO also pointed out the necessity of scientific research in the area of fertility recognition. Research should include: the development of new non-invasive methods of recognizing ovulation in a cycle, the application and effectiveness of methods of recognizing fertility, a multifaceted comparison based on tests of couples who use methods of recognizing fertility and couples who use anti-conception, a study of the factors that motivate couples to choose methods of fertility recognition and the methods to achieve these objectives, the consequences of these methods on the conjugal bond, the connection between the quality of the teaching of these methods of recognition of fertility and their effectiveness, what role the knowledge in the area of recognizing fertility plays in the general attitudes of young people. The results from this fertility research should be utilized in the design of sexual education programs.

"Current knowledge of Natural Family Planning does not leave any doubts and only require thorough adaptation in one's life. Couples that use Natural Family Planning need only basic information that does not require great intellectual pains. Those who are involved professionally with this subject, such as doctors, nurses, midwives, psychologists, family counselors, family life teachers, biologists, catechists, government ministers

(Health and Education), reporters who cover family matters, and instructors of Natural Family Planning, should be more deeply and broadly familiar with the information in this area." (Dr. Urszula Dudziak from the Institute of Family Study KUL, *Knowledge of Natural Family Planning*, 'Nasz Dziennik', p. 25, January 30, 2007).

2. Abuse of One's Sexuality

Unnatural Family Planning Methods

Unnatural family planning methods are among the most serious abuses against God's gift of your sexuality and they are harmful to the mother and the child. They allow for and promote various types of anti-conception (including barrier and early abortive methods). In the event these methods fail and fertilization occurs, abortion is used, which kills the child inside the mother's womb (*abortus* – to be thrown out of the mother's womb, and consequently deprived of life).

1. Anti-conception – (derives from two Latin words *anti* – against and *conceptio* – conception) is the planned effort to prevent the conception of a child during sexual intercourse between man and woman with the help of various methods: chemical, mechanical, hormonal, interruption of sexual intercourse and even the continued use of Natural Family Planning.

Using mechanical and chemical anti-conception may cause a woman to lose her ability to conceive permanently and later efforts to conceive may be overshadowed by fear and doubt. Other side effects include: bleeding, ectopic pregnancy outside, rupturing of the uterus, miscarriage, hormonal imbalance, children born with physical disabilities, etc. (proof comes in the form of many cases before US courts suing for damages). The moral and psychological effects are also disastrous. The wife becomes an object for her husband to use during intercourse instead of a partner. The conscious use of contraception by a couple is a sin because it excludes cooperation with God the Creator, the Giver of Life and His plan for natural order. It takes a negative toll on the religious life of the married couple. Confession will not resolve all issues.

In addition to this, anti-conception methods do not offer a 100 percent guarantee and are less effective than natural methods. They have also been proven to cause damage in the following spheres:

- *biological* (effects of chemicals in the woman's body, multiple pregnancy or permanent infertility);
- *psychological* (a person realizes that he or she is being treated like an object to "use and be used," instead of a partner during marital sex; using contraception slowly kills off one's sensitivity toward the other person's needs during sex);
- *religious* (stifles the conscience, it introduces an ethical disarray and behavior that is against the moral teaching of the Catholic Church which defends the dignity of the human person – the man, as well as, the woman).

"According to data from the Institute of Demographic Studies, 40 years after the passing of Neuwirth's Law legalizing anti-conception in France, 36% of pregnancies are accidental, among these, 26% are unwanted. These numbers clearly demonstrate that the arguments put forth by supporters of contraception – that contraception would help with planning births and would lessen the number of abortions – have been toppled. Although 60% of women between the ages of 20-40 years of age use anti-conception pills, (in 1970, there were only 5%), the number of abortions in France, from year to year, has risen. In 2004, there were 768 thousand live births, and as many as 210 thousand abortions carried out." ("Nasz Dziennik", number 278, November 28, 2007)

2. Sterilization – is among the unnatural and harmful methods of anti-conception, since it permanently mutilates the body of the man or the woman with the goal of making them infertile, incapable of conceiving a new life and therefore becoming a father or mother.

3. Abortion – the greatest enemy of human beings. Abortion is a symbol of the culture of death that dominates the mindset of many people, even in countries where there are low birth rates. It is also strongly propagated by feminist groups with connections to the United Nations, as one of the forms of regulating births (especially in some European Union countries, Africa and China) and by the liberal media which demands that there should be universal access to abortion for every mother, as well as legal protection for the enormous profits of doctors who perform this procedure against a baby in the mother's womb – the most helpless of all human beings.

Reasons for having an abortion are varied: attempts to cover up the consequences of sexually active girls, women or wives, psychological pressure from others (even husbands and fathers) on the mother, or in unusual situations, hatred toward the child that will demand sacrificial love and care.

The effects of abortion are tragic, because it is the murder (a planned killing) of the most innocent of human beings – after conception, but before birth. It is worth viewing pictures of a human being during its various stages of development inside of the mother's womb. They show that the child is not a "blob" of tissue, or undefined group of cells, but rather, a living, beautiful human being.

Consequences of Abortion:
- *Physical* – the death of the child and mutilation of the mother (approx. 25% of women become infertile);
- *Psychological* – a prolonged and deep guilt in the mother (often in the father as well) that may last for years;
- *Spiritual* – a mortal sin "that cries out to heaven" for revenge, a tortured conscience remains until the end of one's life, regardless of confession and absolution.

Josh McDowell reports alarming statistics about some of the consequences of abortion:

- 96% of women are convinced that abortion is the murder of a child;
- 81% of women continue think about their aborted child;
- 73% remember the moment of the abortion;
- 72% of women, even if they were not religious when they had the abortion, later experienced difficulties with their conscience;
- 69% experience mental illness;
- 54% experience nightmares;
- 35% have dreams and visions of their dead child;
- 23% hallucinate related to the abortion;
- women who are believers have a great sense of the sin of abortion;
- many women suffer from post-abortion syndrome, even after giving birth to another child, or infertility after the abortion: for many years they lose the of meaning in life, they become depressed, feel a repulsion toward sexual intercourse, experience powerful phobias and "hear" sounds of a child, they lose their self-esteem, carry the sin (regardless of confession) and through the years, live with a terrible, guilty conscience and bitterness. (M. Rys, *Sexual Intercourse*, "Powiernik Rodzin", 9/1997).

These are only some of the effects. You must remember that the killing of a child by abortion has consequences that reach into the afterlife, so this is no joke!

Anti-conception during Marriage

Using anti-conception during marriage weakens marital love, leads to the "using" of the husband's or the wife's body as an object, changes the biological process in a woman, takes away authentic joy and dignity, makes sex into something mechanical where going through the motions becomes boring, results in conflicts, tension, neurosis, miscarriage, disease, even death, and if it is not effective – it can lead to the killing of an unborn child through abortion. There are disastrous physical, emotional and spiritual side effects from the use of anti-conception, especially for the woman. The natural order, established by God cannot be cheated. This behavior will, sooner or later, be paid for by the woman with a great price in her physical, psychological, biological, or religious life.

In Poland, about 20 percent of couples are infertile, "in large part due to the effects of using anti-conception." Apart from this, the earlier anti-conceptive hormonal manipulation is used, the greater the side effects in the future. A woman using anti-conception under the age of 24 is a "potential candidate for breast, uterus, nipple and skin cancer, as well as many forms of liver disease. Furthermore, it can lead to tumors in the ovaries or cysts. It often contributes to mental disorders, such as depression, as well as, lowers the sex drive".

According to Ewa Obertynska-Romanowska (from the National Panel for the Promotion of Natural Family Planning in Krakow), medical research proves that tampering with the natural order of your body leads to dramatic consequences: "If you want to start taking "the pill" now, your ovaries will not function properly later. Statistics show that about 2 percent of women who took "the pill" will never become pregnant." Obertynska-Romanowska also wrote about the negative effects of anti-conception pills on the heart and circulatory system, as well as, the brain and nervous system.

According to Dr. Hanna Wujkowska (bioethic, advisor for families during the government of Kazimierz Marcinkiewicz), the promotion of anti-conception is aimed at destroying families and marital fidelity. It is important to note that in its very definition, anti-conception is an action against conception; it is the destruction of the human organism's natural function of fertility, as well as, "a battle with one's health, since fertility is a sign of a healthy person." In her estimation, anti-conception is "barbarism, and doctors who participate in it are contradicting the fundamental vocation of a human being and

and their own vocation as doctors." Although they act on the principle of: *primum non nocere* – first, do no harm, when prescribing anti-conception, doctors "hurt" a person's health with full premeditation.

A specific summary of the destructive problems of anti-conception in marriage can be found in title of an article by Magdalena M. Stawarska: *Anti-conception fosters divorce* (*Antykoncepcja sprzyja rozwodom*), "Nasz Dziennik," number 15, January 18, 2007.

It is also known that women need a longer period of time than their husbands to become sexually mature in their marriage, however, they become fundamentally more faithful than their husbands. Men are more spontaneous in their decision to become fathers than their wives, who take put great thought into deciding on motherhood (since women have a greater sense of responsibility for new life and a child's upbringing).

Pornography

Since pornography has become a common phenomenon, it has become the subject of sociological, psychological, pedagogical, psychiatric, and even criminal research. It has caused the rise of many negative phenomena: deterioration of morality, destruction of the human person as a beautiful child of God, limiting the value of the human person to an object of sexual desire, sexual promiscuity, killing of unwanted babies in their mother's womb, sexual crimes, aggression toward children (boys and girls) and women, homosexual activity (of both men and women), the fall of moral sexual ethics, marital and family problems (divorce and the breakup of families), difficulty in raising children and youth, pedophilic behavior, sexual addiction, masturbation in both men and women, feeling a loss of freedom to the point of addiction, molestation and destruction of children and youth (sexual, psychological, moral), the right to defile others in the name of freedom without any legal responsibility, the promotion of deviated attitudes, an increase in sex mania and diseases of erotic mania, the promotion of marital infidelity (first as thoughts, then desires, finally in extramarital sexual acts), violence during sex, vulgarity, mental illness pertaining to sex, lack of respect toward the sexuality of the other person, the marketing of the act, exhibitionism, sadism, masochism, fetishism, rape of children and adults involving murder to cover up the crime, sex with corpses, animals, sex without any obligation and consequence, legalization of prostitution, an increase in sexually transmitted diseases, alcoholism and drugs that increase sexual excitement and weaken another person's self-control or renders them unconscious in order to take advantage of them (rape).

Beneath all of this lies the tragedy of millions of people. Every kind of pornography is a strike against the dignity of the human person. According to the National Catholic Register (49/2006, p.13), every year, profits from the pornographic industry reach 4 to 10 billion dollars. There are 1,300,000 pornographic internet sites used by over 32 million people (data from September 2003). Pornography is the main topic of interest on the internet, yet only three percent of these sites require age verification to prove that the user is an adult. Over 70 percent of young people visit these sites on occasion right after school (when their parents are still at work). Over 60 percent of these sites are sexually explicit (!), and many of them have misleading, innocent titles. The pornography industry (printed material, films, music, clubs, anti-conception, abortion pills) take advantage of people's weaknesses and profit unimaginably from them.

American psychological research has demonstrated the negative effects of pornography (www.life.net.pl), for example:

- Professor Victor B. Cline (University of Utah – 1992) treated 240 patients (96% men) – in almost all the cases pornography caused or contributed to sexual deviation: escalation, loss of sensitivity, acting out of fantasy in real life;

- Professor Dolf Zillman and psychologist Doctor Jennings Bryant of the University of Houston noticed that under the influence of pornography, married couples became dissatisfied with their sex lives, women did not want to have children, and a growing acceptance of sexual promiscuity appeared among both men and women;
- A Canadian psychologist Doctor William Marshall determined that 87% of child molesters who victimized girls, 77% who victimized boys, and 86% of rapists, regularly used pornographic material; of these 57% acted out scenes that they had viewed.

American police officers noticed the connection between the number of rapes committed and the number of pornographic magazines sold. Five times more magazines were sold in Alaska and Nevada than in North Dakota. In these former two states, six times more rapes were reported. Do not think pornography (supposedly only found in special stores "for adults") is not destructive. Court documents pertaining to divorce, violence and drugs show a painful and tragic truth. During an interview with the American psychologist James Dobson, he referred to the words of 42-year-old Ted Bundy, rapist and serial killer of many women:

> I was a normal person (...). I wasn't a pervert in the sense that people look at somebody and say, "I know there's something wrong with him." I was a normal person. I had good friends. I led a normal life, except for this one, small but very potent and destructive segment that I kept very secret (...). As diligent as my parents were, and they were diligent in protecting their children, and as good a Christian home as we had, there is no protection against the kinds of influences that are loose in a society that tolerates (...). In prison (...) I've met a lot of men who were motivated to commit violence. Without exception, every one of

them was deeply involved in pornography - deeply consumed by the addiction. [Without pornography,] I know it would have been far better, not just for me, but for a lot of other people - victims and families (...). I take full responsibility for all the things that I've done. The issue is how [pornography] contributed and helped mold and shape the kinds of violent behavior. It fueled [my] fantasies (...). I don't want to die; I won't kid you. I deserve, certainly, the most extreme punishment society has. And I think society deserves to be protected from me and from others like me. That's for sure. What I hope will come of our discussion is that I think society deserves to be protected from itself. As we have been talking, there are forces at loose in this country, especially this kind of violent pornography, where, on one hand, well-meaning people will condemn the behavior of a Ted Bundy while they're walking past a magazine rack full of the very kinds of things that send young kids down the road to being Ted Bundys (...). There is no way in the world that killing me is going to restore those beautiful children to their parents and correct and soothe the pain. (Life on the Edge, Dr. James Dobson, Copyright © 1995 Word Publishing, Nashville, Tennessee)

What a pain-filled confession. Will you support the pornographic industry, which destroys marriages, children, and other adults? Do not ever say that pornography is not bad! Do we need more tragic evidence?

I walked out of 3 grocery stores owned by Poles living in Guelph, Ontario, and I never went back inside again. I was disgusted by the sight of magazines that were contrary to the teachings of the Catholic Church. I shared my reaction with my parishioners. Other than one person, I did not see the owners and employees of these stores at church. I canceled their ad in the parish bulletin (even though we needed funds for the renovation of the church). My reaction was met with surprise by many people who did not understand the problem.

What will you do about the problem of pornography which is available practically everywhere: in stores, in the movies, at the library, in bookstores, on the internet and so on? In Poland, criminal law is soft, though it provides punishments (202 Penal Code) for those who produce and distribute pornography. There are also not enough people who, seeing the widespread availability of this material in public places, respond in the appropriate way by notifying authorities about these offenses. The Constitution of Poland speaks of the protection of family, marriage, and concerns itself with the proper upbringing of the young generation. Protect yourself and others from pornography and do not be indifferent to its great harm.

Infidelity

When discussing marital infidelity, people often think about sexual infidelity. However, one should notice that infidelity among sacramentally married couples starts earlier, in the spheres of... faith and religious practice (neglecting prayer and the Holy Sacraments, especially during various stressful situations). It starts, thus, with unfaithfulness towards God.

In consequence, in a woman, infidelity first appears on an emotional level, and in a man, in situations where opportunities for cheating arise. After many failed attempts to improve her relationship with her husband and long-term experience of emotional pressure, a wife, feeling helpless, may decide to get involved in a seemingly "meaningless" flirt or romance with another man. A prolonged crisis with her husband can push her to take further steps in infidelity, which will cumulate by involving her emotionally and sexually. Consequently, all of this may lead to separation and civil divorce.

This process takes a different course in a man. When he does not find acceptance in his wife or has constant "noise and messiness" in his home, the temptation increases that another attractive woman will "catch his eye." The process, which begins when he starts to fantasize about her without her knowledge, quickly leads to infidelity in the form of meetings for coffee, for a drink, and later, intentionally, for sex. He can back out faster and more easily than she can, since she becomes more fully involved with the new relationship. However, the wife will forgive her husband more easily, if she still loves him, while the husband will often not want to admit his own guilt and will not want to forgive.

There are many different reasons for marital infidelity. It can be caused by the feeling being rejected by one's spouse, revenge for the unfaithfulness of the other spouse, taking advantage of your own or another person's moment of weakness (sleepiness, too much alcohol, or the influence of drugs, etc.). The liberal media often promotes "free love" without responsibility. Yet there is a great price for unfaithfulness. Regardless of the reason, infidelity is always a betrayal of someone whom you vowed to stay faithful to and of God, in front of whom you made this vow. It is always a sin.

The first effect of infidelity is a guilty conscience, which can even lead neurosis, especially if a spouse was incorrectly suspected of and accused of infidelity and revenge was a mistake with destructive consequences. Other effects of infidelity include sexually transmitted diseases (including HIV and AIDS), unplanned pregnancy (often ending in abortion to cover up the affair), mental illness, as well as, civil divorce and the tragedy of broken families (especially women and their children).

A Moment of Reflection and Dialog

1. Think about and discuss what should be more important in a marriage: sexual freedom without responsibility or authentic love?
2. When and how many children do you want to have in your marriage?
3. Remember that all sexual intercourse between a married couple should to be preceded by (during the day) acts of love and mutual respect. Also it cannot be a forced act, i.e. "you are my spouse, so you must."
4. Both of you, as parents, should involve yourselves in raising your children together since they are the fruit of your married love.

V. Being a Holy Person

God created the human person in His image and likeness as a man and a woman – equal to each other yet different from one another. He directed them to multiply and to take dominion over the earth: "Be fruitful and multiply: fill the earth and subdue it;" (Gen 1:28). Their state of friendship with God and their happiness ended the moment they sinned against God by disobedience. Satan not only tricked Adam and Eve but remained the eternal enemy of all humankind. Even though God punished Adam and Eve, He did not take away their ability to regain happiness. God's merciful love for His people is visible throughout the Old Testament, as are His endless efforts to bring them back to Him. God chose a People, so that through them He could complete His work of the Incarnation and Salvation of all people. Then, through the Church, He continued His plan of gathering and uniting all people with Himself and each other through Jesus Christ. *In this way the love of God was revealed to us: God sent his only Son into the world so that we might have life through him* . (1 Jn 4:9). The Son of God, who became Man by the power of the Holy Spirit, in the marriage of the Virgin Mary and Joseph, through His suffering and death united us with God and all humanity into one Family of God.

Jesus Christ and Mary, His Mother, were invited to the wedding in Cana in Galilee; not only did they celebrate with the couple, but they also helped the newlyweds. It was at this wedding that they first revealed their special concern for married couples. It was there that Jesus, upon the urgent request of Mary, His Mother, performed His first miracle, turning water into wine. This miracle saved both the young couple as well as their merry guests from the first embarrassment in their new life together. The young couple and the steward of the wedding were not even aware that a miracle had been performed. Only the servants who were serving the wine knew that a few moments earlier it had been water.

Christ established the Church as the Family of God, in order to keep helping marriages and families. The couple that invites Jesus to their wedding receives a specific blessing for their new sacramental life together at the altar. This new marriage, as a community of faith and love in Jesus Christ, creates a domestic Church. It is a sign of the presence of Jesus in the world of marriage and family. He joins the couple at the altar and through His presence makes them holy in through their everyday life. The couple is a visible sign of the Sacrament of Marriage, and Christ is its invisible Participant – God. For the Sacrament of Marriage to be valid certain criteria must be fulfilled, as established in the law of the Catholic Church (more information in Chapter VIII, Selected Issues).

A. Faith

1. Natural

Faith is a natural human necessity. Without faith, it would not be possible to live in society. We have faith that the time reported on the radio is correct. Even a small child has faith that his mother and father are truly his parents. We cannot confirm everything, so we accept many things "by having faith." It happens that we may later find we were deceived. Sometimes a wife or a husband, or even parents, consciously allow themselves to be deceived, in order to keep someone from leaving or because they are powerless. A person cannot live without natural faith in his daily life. Sometimes, however, a person who has faith or believes in others, can come to believe he "has been had," or simply, deceived. He cannot always search for the truth; he may not even want to. This kind of natural faith in the authority of can easily - and often does - disappoint. After being deceived, a person may lose their trust – not only in the person who lied to them, but in all people and even in God.

2. Supernatural

Supernatural faith is based on the authority of God Himself, whose love for humankind created them, saved them and to whom He revealed Himself in the most perfect way, through His Son Jesus Christ. Supernatural faith is a conscious acceptance of the sanctifying presence and action of Jesus through His sacraments, which are administered in the Catholic Church. Supernatural faith is rational. It is justified in natural reality, though sometimes it requires a temporary blind faith in God. God, through many different signs, confirms the truth of this Revelation. Supernatural faith is not a part of empirical study; it cannot be verified by experiment. Almighty God lowers Himself to the human level, so that we may accept the revealed truth. God reveals Himself through miracles – factual events that are completely inexplicable, even using the best methods and scientific instruments. Many books have been published on this subject, for example, the Eucharistic miracles, the Mother of God, miracle healings, and so on. They contain photographs, statements and descriptions of events that are impossible to explain in human terms.

Christians do not look for hard, scientific proof that Jesus is present in the sacraments – though Jesus confirmed them many times. He never deceived man. It is worth entrusting yourself and your daily life to Him completely!

Supernatural faith is essential in sacramental life. This is a faith in Jesus Christ, who is present in and sanctifies through the sacraments. Only a person of faith will be able to take advantage of the sanctifying and helping grace that Christ gives through the Sacraments of the Church.

A husband and wife need natural and supernatural faith, to believe in the presence of Christ in the Sacrament of Marriage and in their daily lives, in their marriage, as well as, in His presence in the sacramental husband and the sacramental wife. Whatever the husband does for his wife or the wife does for her husband – they not only do for each other, but also for Christ.

Offending one's wife or husband means offending Christ as well, since He is present in both of them. A human being's essential worth lies in the fact that he was created in the image and likeness of God, and then redeemed by Jesus Christ. If a person is worthy of the love of God, should their spouse not love them unequivocally as well? God sees a person worthy of His love. How then can one spouse be blind, and close his heart to do evil things instead of loving his spouse? It is important for the sacramental couple to try to remember this and ask themselves: do I love my husband or wife as a person? Do I love Jesus who is present in my Sacrament of Marriage? Do I remember that by offending my wife or husband I am offending Jesus as well? Am I aware, that when I offend God, for example, by neglecting my faith (prayer, Reconciliation and Penance, Eucharist), I am also offending my spouse? The Sacrament of Marriage obligates faithfulness towards the person we wed, as well as towards God, in whose presence we were wed. Unfaithfulness to a person is also unfaithfulness to God and unfaithfulness to God is unfaithfulness to a person. This awareness would help sacramental couples avoid much bitterness and instead, give them more joy.

A person with living supernatural faith is a person worthy of trust, a person who loves God in others, and a person who sees God and His will in everyday life. A person whose faith is alive does not seek out and worship the gods of this world. A person whose faith is alive will – despite temptations – endure by God's side, and if he falls, he will seek reconciliation with God and others. Fill yourselves with supernatural faith. Ask Jesus, as the apostles did: Lord, *increase our faith* (Lk 17:5).

In the evening, when examining your conscience, ask yourself: Did I see Jesus in my spouse today? Did I see God in others and in the world around me today? Did I respect His presence? What did the Lord teach me today at home, at work, in school, in the store, on the street and so on? We learn to see God in our joys and sorrows, in sickness and in health – in every situation of life and in every person, and most especially in those who God puts on our path of marriage, family or work as a gift and a calling...

A person whose supernatural faith is alive is filled with peace, because he believes in God's active care over him in every moment of his married, family, working and religious life.

A person whose supernatural faith is alive is can love in situations where, in human terms, it is impossible to love.

We ask God for eyes that are filled with supernatural faith and hearts that are filled with love.

Three thoughts about supernatural faith:

1. If a person does not live as he believes (in God), then he will believe as he lives (he will make up his own religion of "preference," like a supermarket, where he can pick what he likes, justifying his life to himself, to others and in this way falsifying and killing his own conscience). A human cannot stand internal emptiness in the sphere of religion. In writing this, I warn of the tragic consequences in the eternal dimension. This kind of religion does not assure eternal salvation, which is the main goal of human existence. One must accept the whole of Jesus the Savior and all of His Gospels, and not just a selection of attractive statements from the "prophets" of this world, who promise a virtual, not a realistic world.

2. An even worse denial of supernatural faith is the perverse statement that God bestows more blessings upon couples that are married only in a civil union, instead of the Sacramental couple. Of course, God, as the Creator, works together with His creation, which humans are – for their good. However, civil unions do not possess the supernatural grace of a life in friendship with God. Although God loves us and does not take away our free will, He cannot love the sins of those that call themselves Catholics or Christians.

3. The source of supernatural faith is God, who reveals Himself in His works and in His word. His Revelation

was brought together in the Holy Scriptures, or the Bible. God's fullest revelation can be found in the person of Jesus Christ, who God the Father sent as His Only Son, in order to unite all of his people with Him.

It is worth buying the Bible and reading it at home. When you purchase a Bible, make sure it is the Catholic edition. Every translation of the Bible approved by the Catholic Church has the following important inscriptions on its first pages: NIHIL OBSTAT (which means nothing against) and IMPRIMATUR (approved). Why should you buy this version? You should buy this version because the Church, with its authority, seeks to points out an accurate text, thus protecting its members from falsifications of the Word of God and incorrect translations based on inaccurate texts. The Catholic Church through the Magisterium of the Church in its full authority, thanks to the Holy Spirit, interprets the revelation they received from God. This is a great treasure and wondrous gift. It is sad, but not every edition of the Holy Bible contains an accurate text. We experienced this throughout the history of Christianity and we are experiencing this now.

Besides having a copy of the Holy Bible in every home, there should also be a copy of the *Catechism of the Catholic Church* or at least it's *Compendium*. Both books are the basic and essential sources of your own religious knowledge and are helpful in your discussions with others. They were not only written for theologians, but for all people of faith. It is good to have both the full version and the shortened version of the *Catechism*. After the Catechism of Trent (XVI century), this is the first publication that takes into account the entire official teaching of the Catholic Church, as accepted by Pope John Paul II. This Catechism quickly became a best seller all over the world, purchased not only by Catholics, but also by non-Catholics, as well as, by non-Christians. In working on increasing your supernatural faith, it is good to find time to study the rudiments of our faith – the best time being on Sunday after lunch or dinner.

B. The Holy Sacraments in Engagement and Marriage

There are seven sacraments that sanctify a person in the Catholic Church: Baptism, Eucharist, Reconciliation, Confirmation, Anointing of the Sick, Holy Orders and Marriage. They are essential in the spiritual development of a person, so that he may be able to live a holy life on earth, as well as, attain their ultimate goal of salvation and everlasting life with God. From the moment of Baptism, a Christian is a child of God and a brother or sister to Jesus Christ. During Baptism, Christ brings a person into the life of God within the Holy Trinity. This supernatural gift of becoming a child of God also requires supernatural grace (help) for continued development. Thanks to this grace, a person may offer their whole world to God, as it is a gift from the Creator and the place of human pilgrimage to the House of the Father.

1. The Sacrament of Baptism

The first and fundamental Sacrament is Baptism. It washes away all sins (first, original sin – inherited from Adam and Eve, the first parents, and a part of the lives of all human beings thereafter), unites us with God in the Church community and impresses a mark on the soul that is irremovable. Through Baptism, a person receives a special gift and the seeds of virtues of faith, hope and love that are given to help in one's life with God. Engaged couples and Spouses should remind themselves that once, in their names, their parents and godparents, made promises to God and took up the responsibility of helping the newly baptized to fulfill these Christian vows in their daily lives.

During the Baptism of their child, a married couple has the perfect opportunity to renew their own Baptismal promises and thank God for their parents and godparents, as well as, everyone who helped them "grow in grace of God and other people." Participating in the Baptism of their children, they should understand that now they take responsibility before God and the Church community for their children's spiritual and religious lives, until their own life ends. The married couple, as parents, should seek help in completing this great, honorable and responsible task. They should select godparents who fully practice the Catholic faith and who will ask God for the necessary graces for the child, as well as, the parents, and not chose people because they are wealthy friends. The spiritual wealth of the godparents is without a doubt more important than material wealth. It is worth remembering that thanks to the grace of Baptism, we are immersed in the death of Christ, so as to spiritually rise with Him into a new life. By being one Family of God, we are responsible for the salvation of everyone in this Family. Spouses have a much greater responsibility toward one another before God than they do towards others, even their own children. From the moment of the Holy Baptism, Christ longs to live within each person as his brother or sister and child of God. Therefore the life of a Christian should be a reflection of Jesus' life. The converted Saul, as St. Paul, Apostle of Nations, experienced this unity in a wondrous way: *yet I live, no longer I, but Christ lives in me (Gal 2:20)*.

2. The Sacrament of Confirmation

A maturing young person needs special help from God, so that the miraculous gifts he received at Baptism can continue to develop. The three sacraments of Baptism, Confirmation and Eucharist lead a person toward the road of friendship with God, help him to grow and be like Christ. Engaged and married couples need the gifts of the Holy Spirit in order to grow into responsible Catholics. That is why engaged Catholics should receive the Sacrament of Confirmation before receiving the Sacrament of Marriage. All of the gifts of the Holy Spirit empower husbands and wives to build and develop their marriage as a Catholic, Sacramental community of faith and love.

Maybe you have already forgotten about the gifts and the fruits of the Holy Spirit. Maybe they, as only seeds, were thrown into the hard rock of your souls, overwhelmed by the events of this world and that is why they have not yet bore fruit. Now is the time to talk about them together. Now is the time to ask the Holy Spirit to renew them in your hearts and in your lives. Only the Spirit which Jesus sent to sanctify the Church during the time of apostles can sanctify you as engaged and married couples.

It is the Holy Spirit, who through His gifts (wisdom, knowledge, counsel, courage, understanding, reverence, and holy fear of the Lord) and the fruits (patience, kindness, goodness, gentleness, faithfulness, modesty, self-control, love, joy and peace) will help your inner development. He will help you grow and accomplish the tasks God has given you as an engaged couple, as a married couple and as parents. He will empower you to realize your vocation in this difficult, modern world.

3. The Sacrament of Reconciliation and Penance

We know about the imperfections and sinfulness of the humans through our own personal experiences and through contact with others. An awareness of our own weakness and tendency to do wrong should lead us to look for help, in order to become free ourselves from evil and our tendency toward it, as well as to be more inclined to do good. Experiencing our own evil and weakness, should allow us to better understand weaknesses of other people. This gift of understanding is important in the lives of engaged and married couples, especially when loved ones discover each other's flaws. This gift helps you to be more understanding and forgiving, but also requires a change for the better on both sides. Your own example of love and forgiveness really does work miracles.

For 18 years, St. Monica prayed and offered her suffering to God and finally before her death, she was able to witness the conversion of her husband and her son, Augustine, who became a Saint. She died, smiling, in the arms of her weeping son. She is buried in the Church of St. Augustine in Rome.

There are various people and institutions that can help you become a better person. Jesus Christ gave us the most effective assistance: Himself as the Doctor of people's souls through the Sacrament of Reconciliation and Penance. There is no psychologist or psychiatrist that can help a married couple more. Of course, they may - from a psychological perspective - enlighten the couple about how the human mechanism works which leads to doing what is right or wrong, but they can never free a person from the guilt of a consciously and freely committed evil act (sin). In situations where engaged or married couples purposely hurt and attack each other, it is especially necessary – though difficult, but such a blessing – for them to reach out to the Sacrament of Reconciliation and Penance. A good confession received by the spouses increases their supernatural faith, protects their faithful love, gives them grace, makes them more sensitive to evil, gives them strength to endure, develops their awareness of the Lord and their spouse, increases their eagerness in attending to their daily duties, gradually washes away their egoism, increases their respect for God and people, allows their heart to be more delicate, helps them to forgive each other, gives a greater sense of freedom, deepens their ability to understand each other, calms the soul, effectively destroys the roots of addiction, overcomes the presence of Satan in their married sacramental life and so on.

Couples who take their faith seriously will tell often you, "whenever difficulties and misunderstandings arise between us, we go first to Confession and Communion, and later our problems seem to disappear." Reconciliation and Penance is the most necessary sacrament for married couples, as well as engaged couples, helping them to persevere and grow in their love as husband and wife. This is because this Sacrament returns purity to the soul, as well as, our friendship with God and between people. Afterward, in Holy Communion, Jesus strengths and develops the love of the engaged and married couples.

Both sides, in order to acknowledge their guilt, need to look deep inside through an examination of their own conscience. This examination should be based on the realities of life and involve matters regarding their engagement or marriage as well as those of being parents (if they are). Only then, when they have accepted their own guilt, felt remorse and the need for mutual forgiveness, as well as a need for the forgiveness of God, can they make an honest confession. This, however, is not the end of the matter.

They should also find a way to put right the things they did wrong toward God and others, in order to receive the essential grace (God's help) for an even deeper faithfulness and more beautiful engaged or married life with respect and mutual love.

Afterwards, individually, though with mutual support for one another, they should carry out their penance by making a change in their lives (turning away from the cause of the sin and doing good), because both of them benefit from the fruits of the Sacrament of Reconciliation and Penance. This Sacrament helps them both to understand that even though they are very important in the relationship, Jesus Christ is the most important one in their lives. He is the one who joins them together and wants to live in their hearts and minds, so that they can make God's decisions in their everyday lives. Changing your life, even in the smallest way, is most essential after confession; it is an external sign of true sorrow for sin and inner renewal. That kind of change helps you to be a better person, fiancé or sacramental spouse, and child of God.

The Sacrament of Reconciliation and Penance is wonderful medicine for the problems encountered in engaged life and a special healing balm in the lives sacramentally married couples. A truly deep and regular experience of this sacrament by both fiancés and spouses is a guarantee of their real spiritual development. The "psychological cost" is very small compared to the renewal and the spiritual unification that comes to the couple afterwards. The role of a tough "prosecutor" and self-accusation by confessing your own sins in this sacrament does not make you a victim, but rather, gives you victory over the evil that is within you and over Satan, its active accomplice. It is he who is the greatest enemy of humans, battling against them in a double-crossing war, under "the banner" of alleged freedom and false good and, in this way, striving to destroy the bond with Christ in every soul and every heart. Even upon the ruins of human weakness, God can build a wonderful spiritual palace unifying the bodies and souls of fiancés or spouses. Their input into the practicing of this sacrament brings countless benefits to both of them.

Three very important things:
1. Choose a good priest as your confessor and pray for him to the Holy Spirit (especially before confession), so that representing God's will, he can help you through his priestly service.
2. The more the confession will cost you inside, the more grace you will receive from God, who is filled with Loving Mercy.
3. A good confession will save you a lot of inner tension, as well as, a lot of money, which could otherwise be spent on trying to save your engagement, marriage or family with the help of lawyers and judges, psychologists and psychiatrists.

4. The Sacrament of the Anointing of the Sick

Times of illness are a difficult exam for the person who is ill as well as those around him, especially when treatment is expensive, the sick person requires 24-hour assistance and is lonely in his suffering. A long illness can deplete the physical and psychological strength of the sick person and everyone around him. Every illness, especially if it is long and drawn out, is a chance to show love for the sick person, and even more so when he or she is your fiancé or spouse. The sick loved-one has a right to expect help from his fiancé or spouse, but also from Jesus, who should be invited to help through the Sacrament of the Anointing of the Sick. Do not delay in inviting a priest to come and administer this sacrament, since he will be able to help the sick person reunite with God and receive Jesus in Holy Communion. You should not wait to call a priest until the sick person is unconscious and dying. The Sacrament of the Anointing of the Sick strengthens the sick in their illness, not the dead. The dead need a funeral, not anointing. How very often I have witnessed the tears of regret of spouses who did not ask for a priest before their loved ones passed away.

Suffering experienced with Jesus opens a person to share in the mystery of His own saving suffering. A person who is ill is not "unemployed" and useless. He has a great mission within the Church: he can and should offer his suffering to Jesus in the Holy Mass, which is celebrated in every moment in every church or chapel across the world. The time of illness and reha- bilitation is not only a time to worry about returning to physical health, but even more so – it is a time for the rehabilitation of the soul. The soul needs the body to "move away" from every- day issues, so that the person can look at his whole life from a different perspective – one of faith and eternal life. It is the per- fect time to have a "retreat" of the soul with God, so that the sick person can analyze his life up until this moment and look toward the future – which often turns out to be near – of eter- nal life after death.

The beginning of an illness can often be a time of rebel- lion and resentment toward God and everyone else, even to- ward oneself. Then, those who are closest to the sick person should surround him with special care and help raise his spirits. In such moments, prayer for and with the sick person is price- less, especially in the presence of loved ones and a priest. The visit of a priest at this time will help the ill person reunite with God and others through the Sacrament of Reconciliation and

Penance. The sacramental spouse who is ill needs Jesus in the Holy Communion to show him the meaning of his life and illness. The sick – according to Pope John Paul II – are the diamonds of the Church. During his apostolic pilgrimages, John Paul II, as a loving father and pastor of the world, always had time to meet with the sick. This meeting was more helpful to them than were doctors or medicine. It gave them joy and helped them find Jesus in a difficult moment of their lives, as well as, revealed to them the saving sense of their suffering with Christ.

5. The Sacrament of Holy Orders

The Sacraments of Holy Orders (Priesthood) and Eucharist are particularly necessary for the engaged and married couple. The Priest, minister of the Sacraments and guardian of Jesus in the Eucharist, has a very specific role in the lives of engaged and married couples. As the shepherd of their souls, he should help them in a way that is crystal clear, responsible and faithful. He should be the spiritual guide on their way to growing in unity with God and others, as well as, help them to attain holiness in their engagement and marriage.

The gift of Holy Orders is a gift of service given by Jesus Himself for people who need and search for God in their lives. Priests should be especially sensitive to the spiritual needs of engaged and married couples.

Although priests have human needs for intimacy and companionship, this can become an obstacle which makes it more difficult to offer pastoral help and best serve as a priest to the faithful. The priest-pastor, as their spiritual guide, should avoid becoming too familiar with engaged and married couples. The priest should not only offer his warmth and hospitality during pleasant meetings over coffee, by the fireside or at domestic "chapels", but even more so, to those who need his help during difficult times. Engaged and married couples should look for and choose a spiritual guide from among experienced priests, as opposed to someone who is a secular and a pleasant buddy to chat and hang out with.

I remember, some years ago, I was asked to be someone's spiritual director. The requirements I set for this person seemed too difficult. She rejected them. I believed, however, that the issues at stake were too great and too deep to approach casually. When providing spiritual direction, it is the good of the person's soul that is the most important concern of the confessor. His spiritual role is greater than a secular or social point of view. The person receiving this pastoral service, as well as the priest who leads him should remember this. Spiritual guidance is a very difficult and responsible task. It requires maturity and responsibility from both sides, but especially from the priest, or spiritual director. Spiritual guidance cannot become a circle of mutual adoration, but must lead to the adoration of Jesus in the Eucharist and in everyday life, which may be very demanding.

6. The Sacrament of the Eucharistic

The present and living Jesus Christ works through all the sacraments. All of the previously described sacraments should prepare people for the most beautiful and most fulfilling meeting with Jesus in the Eucharist. Every action of engaged and married people during the day or week, should lead to the most joyful moment: OFFERING THEMSELVES TO JESUS AND ACCEPTING HIS BODY AND BLOOD IN HOLY COMMUNION! Holy Communion should be the most wonderful and the most intimate moment of love in the life of a person, especially in the life of people who are engaged or sacramentally married. The Eucharist is the Sacrament of Love. It is Jesus, alive and filled with love. This is why celebrating the Holy Mass together as a couple during the week, and especially on Sunday and Holy Days of obligation, is an unmatched meeting of their human love with the love of God. Engaged and married couples should prepare themselves together for this meeting, so that they can be enrich and sanctify their inner lives, as well as, have their daily life transformed.

a) Participation of Engaged and Married Couples in the Holy Mass

The EUCHARIST is the source of Christian life in marriage. Active and full participation in the Holy Mass demands you to first free your soul from mortal sin (if you are in a state of mortal sin, then you should go to confession *before* going to Holy Mass, so that you can receive Jesus in Holy Communion). You, as engaged or married couples, should bring the individual and common concerns you have in your hearts to this Eucharistic meeting, so as to present them to Christ during the preparation of the gifts. After the consecration of the bread and wine, the priest raises the Body of Christ in the Host and His Blood in the chalice. During this time, you should mutually offer yourselves to Jesus and ask Him to present your offering to God the Father.

The moment of accepting Jesus in Holy Communion should be your mutual – and the most joyous – moment of your day or week. Nothing and no one should replace this experience. During the time of praise and thanks, after receiving Jesus, TOGETHER, as a couple, you should renew the love in your hearts; as a married couple, you should also renew your marital vows and kiss your wedding ring.

After some time as an engaged or married couple, you will begin to experience that Jesus not only loves you, but increases your love for each other. The feeling that Jesus is close to you during the Holy Mass is a beautiful thing; however, do not expect this kind of experience during every Eucharistic celebration. Jesus often manifested Himself in the Eucharist in an unusual way, not only to saints, such as a priest who doubted in the presence of Jesus during consecration (in Bolsena, Italy in the 13th century).

Common prayer with your fellow brothers and sisters in faith will help you find your own religious identity as a domestic church within the local and universal Church. After a long day or week of working and running around, you, as a couple, will rejoice in the experience of belonging to the local community of a parish family and identifying with them.

Then, the Holy Mass will become vital for you, not only because of God's third Commandment, but most importantly due to the inner need of the heart and soul. Holy Mass will gradually become YOUR MEETING WITH GOD WITHIN A COMMUNITY OF FAITH AND LOVE! Jesus will gradually purify and free you, though you are not "angels" and you may feel "covered with ashes or smeared in the mud of this world" (evil).

- Jesus will slowly liberate you, offering you the freedom of God's children and the ability to make a fuller offering of love for one another and others.
- You will gradually understand more fully and feel the need for God's love and each other.
- You will be able to share God's love with every person you meet.
- You will wait in anticipation of your next meeting with Jesus in the Eucharistic Church Community.
- It is Jesus Christ in the Eucharist that will bind you more closely with one another, while the Holy Spirit will sanctify you and give you the gifts that you will need.

For there to be happiness in your engagement and marriage, you need to live with God in your everyday life, as well as, be able to bring all the joys and difficulties of your engagement, marriage and family life to Jesus as a gift. Ask the Holy Spirit to take this gift and purify it, and then ask Jesus to offer it to the Father. The Holy Mass will then become a celebration of your life in Christ and with Christ in every moment.

b) The Parish in the Life of Engaged and Sacramentally Married Couples

Your Parish, or local Church, is the place where the sanctification of the faithful takes place, including for engaged and the sacramentally married couples, within the community of the Universal Church. The local Church organizes special moments of being with God – retreats, meetings for engaged couples, meetings for married couples, pilgrimages, religious education and so on. These different forms of parish ministry should help you grow spiritually as an engaged and married couple.

As fiancés or even more so, married spouses, who desire a deeper union with one another in God, you will feel the need for the help of the priest as a spiritual guide. This is an important and difficult task. Today, it is not easy to find a priest who will take up this kind of spiritual guidance, but if you should find such a priest and he agrees to take on this blessed task, then both of you will receive special graces from God. How wonderful it is to tell someone trusted and close to God, about your spiritual issues. A spiritual guide who authentically lives a life with God, as well as, others, who want to take advantage of his guidance (such as engaged and married couples) will benefit by becoming even closer to God.

Your guide will help you become more in tune with one another and other people. After a certain period of time, God will give you the opportunity to share your experiences with other engaged and married couples. Mutual prayer, first as an engaged couple, later as a married couple, in the church and in your home, will enrich you. In the future, it will prepare your home for the arrival and Catholic development of your children.

7. The Sacrament of Marriage

St. Paul, in his letter to the Ephesians, compares married love between a husband and a wife to the love that Christ has for the Church:

Be subordinate to one another out of reverence for Christ. Wives should be subordinate to their husbands as to the Lord. For the husband is head of his wife just as Christ is head of the church, he himself the savior of the body. As the church is subordinate to Christ, so wives should be subordinate to their husbands in everything.

Husbands, love your wives, even as Christ loved the church and handed himself over for her to sanctify her, cleansing her by the bath of water with the word, that he might present to himself the church in splendor, without spot or wrinkle or any such thing, that she might be holy and without blemish. So (also) husbands should love their wives as their own bodies. He who loves his wife loves himself. For no one hates his own flesh but rather nourishes and cherishes it, even as Christ does the church, because we are members of his body.

"For this reason a man shall leave (his) father and (his) mother and be joined to his wife, and the two shall become one flesh." This is a great mystery, but I speak in reference to Christ and the church. (Eph 5:21-32)

What a wonderful vision: to love in such a way as Christ loves the Church! To love endlessly and to be at someone's disposition in every moment of life. To love in such a way to fulfill our Heavenly Father's will and to remain within this love here on earth and later, eternally with God. To love so much that you are ready to lay your life down for your beloved at any moment. How is it possible not to love such a spouse in return? In this kind of love there is no humiliation or dependence, it is only a personal relationship of mutual, sacrificial love.

I have - from time to time - heard the response of young husbands to the above mentioned text from the Bible. Already, on the day of their wedding, the husbands remind their new wives about obedience. In response to this, I point out their one-sided viewpoint and their tendency to take into account only the part of the text they want to remember. I then ask them, are they ready to lay down their lives for their wives, following the example of Christ? Most often they respond with silence, which is not a positive answer to my question. The love of Christ and the Church, remain the most perfect example of mutual love. I wish this kind of love upon all sacramentally married couples. I know that with this kind of love, they will have everything they need for happiness in this life on earth and in the next life in heaven, since they have Christ and each other in Him. Christ never disappointed the Church, and the Church always loved Christ. The human being is a great mystery to himself and to others. An even greater mystery is the sacramentally married couple - the mystery of the lives of two people united in the Sacrament to become husband and wife. Only the presence of Christ and His assistance can make the mystery of the sacramentally married couple such an effective, great and legible sign of holiness, that the spouses become a catalyst for holiness in their marriage, family and surroundings.

Your prayers and everyday sacramental life as spouses will transform you into a domestic Church, and as you are sanctified, you will help those closest to you in their sanctification and later through your local parish, sanctify and evangelize your surrounding world. Just as no one lives only for themselves, your sacramental marriage is not for you alone. You have a wonderful mission within the Church and the world: to be holy and sanctify others (*sanctificari et sanctificare*).

The Sacrament of Marriage encompasses every moment of your lives as husband and wife, both solemn prayer in Church, as well as, ordinary prayer in your home and beyond. It is therefore not only a sacrament for a certain moments of time, but for one's whole life. It is a sacrament of your conscious life as spouses in Christ, who joined you and strengthens you in the realization of your demanding vocation. You need the presence of Christ in every sacrament. Your bodies and souls, as husband and wife, serve to more perfectly unify and sanctify you in Christ. This sacramental style of life is visible and necessary for you, your children, the Church and the world. As spouses living the Sacrament on a daily basis, you will be renewed and you will help to renew the world around you. Do not be embarrassed to be a living and visible sign of this kind of life. Be grateful to God, the Church and to each other for the gift of a sacramental marriage. It is Jesus who sanctified the everyday life of Mary and Joseph. Growing up among them, He also helped them to grow more fully as a married couple who loved God. You will never be perfect on earth; however, you will strive to perfect yourselves as human beings, spouses, parents, workers, friends, acquaintances, and so on. The Sacrament of Marriage is a most perfect "chisel" in the hand of God, who sculpts His image and likeness into the core of your being. Allow yourselves to be the best living "raw material" at His disposition in every moment of your married lives!

Dear Sacramentally Married Couples! There is one more reason you should pray together and attend weekly Mass together. According to the research of American sociologist Mercedes Arzu Wilson, divorce occurred in 50 percent of couples married only in a civil ceremony; 33 percent of sacramentally married, but non-practicing, couples; 2 percent of sacramentally married couples who regularly attend Sunday Mass, and only 0.07 percent (1 out of 1429 couples) of sacramentally married couples who regularly attend Sunday Mass as well as pray together daily. ("Rycerz Niepokalanej," number 556, September 2002, pg. 289). Can there be greater insurance for a LIFE TOGETHER?! Be thankful to Jesus and the Church for this beautiful gift: the Sacrament of Marriage.

C. Other Liturgical Celebrations

1. The Sacramentals and Popular Piety

In Part Two of the *Catechism of the Catholic Church*, right after the section on the Holy Sacraments, the first article in Chapter Four, entitled, *"Other Liturgical Celebrations"* discusses the Sacramentals, which after the Holy Sacraments, make up the main and most commonly accessible methods of sanctification in a Christian's life.

"Holy Mother Church has, moreover, instituted. These are sacred signs which bear a resemblance to the sacraments.

They signify effects, particularly of a spiritual nature, which are obtained through the intercession of the Church. By them men are disposed to receive the chief effect of the sacraments, and various occasions in life are rendered holy." (nr. 1667)

"Sacramentals derive from the baptismal priesthood: every baptized person is called to be a 'blessing' and to bless. Hence lay people may preside at certain blessings; the more a blessing concerns ecclesial and sacramental life, the more is its administration reserved to the ordained ministry (bishops, priests, or deacons)." (nr. 1669)

"Sacramentals do not confer the graces of the Holy Spirit in the way that the sacraments do, but by the Church's prayer, they prepare us to receive grace and dispose us to cooperate with it. 'For well-disposed members of the faithful, the liturgy of the sacraments and sacramentals sanctifies almost every event of their lives with the divine grace which flows from the Paschal mystery of the sacraments and sacramentals draw their power. There is scarcely any proper use of material things which cannot be thus directed toward the sanctification of men and the praise of God'" (nr. 1670)

"Among sacramentals *blessings* (of person, meals, objects, and places) come first. Every blessing praises God and prays for His gifts. In Christ, Christians are blessed by God the Father 'with every spiritual blessing.' This is why the Church imparts blessings by invoking the name of Jesus, usually while making the holy sign of the cross of Christ." (nr. 1671)

"Certain blessings have a lasting importance because they consecrate persons to God, or reserve objects and places for liturgical use. Among those blessings which are intended for persons – not to be confused with sacramental ordination – are the blessing of the abbot or abbess of a monastery, the consecration of virgins and widows, the rite of religious profession and the blessing of certain ministries of the Church (readers, acolytes, catechists, etc.). The dedication or blessing of a Church, blessing of holy oils, vessels, and vestments, bells, etc., can be mentioned as examples of blessings that concern objects." (nr. 1672)

"When the Church asks publicly and authoritatively in the name of Jesus Christ that a person or object be protected against the power of the Evil One and withdrawn from his dominion, it is called *exorcism*. Jesus performed exorcisms and from Him the Church has received the power and office of exorcising. In a simple form, exorcism is performed at the celebration of Baptism. The solemn exorcism, called 'a major exorcism,' can be performed only by a priest and with permission of the bishop. The priest must proceed with prudence, strictly observing the rules established by the Church. Exorcism is directed at the expulsion of demons or to the liberation from demonic possession through the spiritual authority which Jesus entrusted to His Church. Illness, especially psychological illness, is a very different matter; treating this is the concern of medical science. Therefore, before an exorcism is performed, it is important to ascertain that one is dealing with the presence of the Evil One, and not an illness." (nr. 1673)

"Besides sacramental liturgy and sacramentals, catechesis must take into account the forms of piety and popular devotions among the faithful. The religious sense of the Christian people has always found expression in various forms of piety surrounding that Church's sacramental life, such as the veneration of relics, visits to sanctuaries, pilgrimages, processions, the Stations of the Cross, religious dances, the Rosary, medals, etc." (nr. 1674)

"These expressions of piety extend the liturgical life of the Church, but do not replace it. They 'should be so drawn up that they harmonize with the liturgical seasons, accord with the sacred liturgy, are in some way derived from it and lead the people to it since in fact the liturgy by its very nature is far superior to any of them.'" (nr. 1675)

"Pastoral discernment is needed to sustain and support popular piety and, if necessary, to purify and correct the religious sense which underlies these devotions so that the faithful may advance in knowledge of the mystery of Christ. Their exercise is subject to the care and judgment of the bishops and to the general norms of the Church." (nr. 1676)

Practical Conclusions

The Sacramentals, in the life of the Church, have a very practical and spiritual meaning. They should not be treated as magic, nor devotional objects (like holy medallions) as amulets or simply necklaces. Instead, they should be an exterior expression of an interior religious conviction. The gift of faith, even though it is personal for a given person, can become, in his everyday life – in certain circumstances – the most enriching gift for the community. The faith of one person can sometimes ignite the faith of thousands and millions of people, just as Pope John Paul II or Mother Teresa strengthened the faith of some and helped others to believe.

Spouses should help each other on their road of faith which sanctifies them. The blessed wedding ring on your finger should not only remind you of the joyful moments of your life with Christ, but it should also be a sign (like your whole life should be) for others that you have given yourself to each other and together you have given yourself to Christ. You should never hide it; and it would be good for a husband to kiss his wife and her wedding ring, as well as for the wife to kiss her husband and his wedding ring. Right before the bride and groom put the wedding ring on each other's hands, I ask each of them in turn to first kiss the ring. The wedding ring should also remind you that God is with you always, in order to help you become better and more holy.

A very beautiful image – though unfortunately vanishing – is the sight of a married couple walking arm in arm. It is interesting that before marriage, it was impossible to separate them. They were proud to hold hands or walk arm in arm. What happened afterwards? Would it be possible that they became embarrassed to walk like this with one another? This is also an "unwritten," specific form of "marriage sacramentalium." Spouses! Return to the beautiful forms of expressing your unity. Maybe it will help others find fulfillment in their marriages? Of course walking arm in arm (every time) requires an attitude of mutual love and agreement. Therefore, it would be good to reconcile (if necessary) before leaving the house and walking arm and arm.

Blessing your home, a cross or an image of Jesus or Mary, St. Joseph or other saints (and putting them in a visible place in your home), is a sign of the faith of the people living there. Making **the sign of the cross** on the forehead of your spouse as they are leaving the house or on the forehead of your children - before bed or school – is not only a blessing, but also a collective act of faith.

How sad looking are those crosses that are treated as decorations, the ones that are worn as necklaces by people whose very lives deny the Christian faith; or worse, when people mock Christ and the mostly Christian public allows for it! A house that is blessed should be the dwelling of people who believe and love God and others. **Holy water** placed **near the entrance** of the house should help the people who live there in their battle with evil and Satan. The family should form a domestic church filled with the presence of God, who is Love.

Do not be ashamed **to pray** (without ostentation), to hold a rosary in your hand, to pray before a meal at home or when you are out, as well as, at parties, and public places, for example, in restaurants. I often see practicing Catholics, even priests, who begin their meals without the sign of the cross. Why should you be embarrassed? **The sign of the cross is the sign of our Savior.**

One day a very distraught man came to his priest and said, "Father, I drove in a car that was not blessed and never had an accident. You blessed my car and I had an accident!" The priest answered him, "I blessed the car, not the driver." The blessing of the car was supposed to remind him to abide by the traffic regulations and be a careful, sober driver. It was

not a guarantee of safety when driving too fast or while intoxicated.

The Sacramentals are like a thermometer of the religious
feelings and conviction of people and a society, as well as, for a
sacramentally married couple.

Our Polish religious traditions, especially the domestic
ones, are very rich in Sacramentals. In this regard, we are truly a
wealthy people. This richness amazes Catholics and even non-
Christians especially where Polish people are immigrants. Some
observers even invite themselves to join in on Polish family religious celebrations – especially Wigilia (Christmas Eve dinner) –
and are eager hear about them.

2. The Christian Funeral

"All the sacraments, and principally those of Christian
initiation, have as their goal the last Passover of the child of
God which, through death, leads him into the life of the Kingdom. Then what he confessed in faith and hope will be fulfilled:
'I look for the resurrection of the dead, and the life of the world
to come.'" (nr. 1680)

"For the Christian the day of death inaugurates, *at the end
of his sacramental life*, the fulfillment of his new birth begun at
Baptism, the definitive 'conformity' to 'the image of the Son'
conferred by the anointing of the Holy Spirit, and participation
in the feast of the Kingdom which was anticipated in the Eucharist – even if final purifications are still necessary for him in
order to be clothed with the nuptial garment." (nr. 1682)

"The Christian funeral is a liturgical celebration of the
Church. The ministry of the Church in this instance aims at expressing efficacious communion with *the deceased*, at the participation in that communion of *the community* gathered for the funeral, and at the proclamation of eternal life to the community."
(nr. 1684)

Full participation in a funeral should be a celebration of
eternal life in Christ. This is why one should do everything pos-

sible to make sure that the dying person is reconciled to God and to people before death. Then the funeral, though filled with sadness and pain because of the departure of a loved one, becomes a true celebration and thanksgiving for their life and love. After many centuries of a different tradition, the Church, in certain situations, allows for white liturgical vestments to be used during a funeral – as the color of Paschal joy, even though the color of purple or black would sometimes better communicate the religious state of a deceased person. Tears are wiped away by faith and the belief that the deceased person, regardless of imperfections, truly loved God and others. They become tears of joy and gratitude to God for this person and his life, for example in the case of Pope John Paul II. Full participation in the Holy Mass (essential to celebrate as the main part of the funeral) should be joined by receiving Jesus in Holy Communion and entrusting the deceased person to Him so that He may welcome him at the gate of His Father's Heavenly House.

Yet, how sorrowful is the participation in the funeral of a person who did not want to reconcile with God. It is even more tragic when the deceased person fought – humanly speaking – with God until the end. There are justified situations in which the Church refuses someone who is baptized a Christian funeral or does not allow the coffin to be brought into a church. This happens in specific cases when the dying person definitely rejects God and the Church, and therefore the refusal of the Church simply respects the will of the deceased.

ETERNAL REST, GRANT ONTO THEM, O LORD, AND LET THE PERPETUAL LIGHT SHINE UPON THEM. MAY THEY REST IN PEACE. AMEN.

The Church encourages Holy Masses to be offered for the deceased in order to help them achieve the perfect joy of heaven. Try to take advantage of this form of assistance to offer Holy Masses and receive Holy Communion for your departed loved ones.

D. Prayer

Prayer is the necessary "breath" of spiritual life, so that the heart beats for God and with Him for others. A person discovers his identity when meeting with God, who is Love. Parents, as the first catechists, are responsible for creating a religious environment in their homes and teaching their children to pray. A family that is strong in God is a family that prays together every day. Families such as these – even among Catholics – are far too few. The time youth is also a time of difficult time with prayer. For a young person, the prayers of their childhood are no longer enough, but most often, they are still unfamiliar with other forms of prayer. We should not be surprised that young people do not pray very often or that they simply "escape" from prayer – from both individual prayer, as well as, community prayer – because they do not know how to pray (and embarrassment can paralyze even the best intentions).

Your engagement is a good time to discuss your prayer life now and once you are married. Without prayer, which is a sign of faith, it is not possible to develop your holiness. You cannot change the past – you can change the future. This is why as engaged couples, spouses, and families, you should pray together – if you want to grow spiritually, and achieve holiness and joy in your life together.

Once, in Sterling Heights (18 miles from Detroit), I met an engaged couple, who came to me after the wedding of their friends (who were Polish) and asked if I would agree to bless their marriage. They were both Americans as well as students from Toledo, Ohio. Due to the distance, I asked them to come to me with their papers after they finished their marriage preparation class in their parish or at the university. They came. During the meeting I asked them which of the classes they liked the best. To my surprise they said, the teachings about prayer. After that class, they began to pray together. The prayer they began together brought them even closer. They passed on their experience to their married friends. When they started to pray as well, it helped them to experience an even greater unity; their love for each other also grew.

Join prayer should begin during your engagement and continue into your married life.

How do we Start Praying Together?

At first, block off a period of time to pray together in "silence" and in this silence ask the Holy Spirit for help. After this moment is completed, you can use a prayer book, pray the Rosary, a litany, the prayers of the Holy Mass and so on. Never hurry over the words of verbal prayer. During prayer, do not talk over God. Give God a chance to speak to you in the silence of your heart. Find time to go to Adoration of the Blessed Sacrament or to adore Jesus in the tabernacle at your parish. Before you commit to saying the prayer you have chosen, try to understand the meaning of every word that will be said and then look at what the whole prayer is trying to communicate. Do not be afraid to write your own prayer and recite it. You can modify or perfect it with time. Once praying has a grip on you and you start to delight in "being with God," you will notice that you will say less to Him as you listen to Him more.

Then you will notice that you are talking to Him in your heart and you are beginning to – truly – rejoice that you are with Him!

Courage! This is possible and so very joyful!

In 1980, I visited a little place in France called Ars. St. John Vianney (19th century), the patron of priests, lived and worked as a pastor there. He served as confessor to people for hours and hours every day. Once, as he was sitting in the confessional, he saw a man in his little parish church, who came in and stood by the door. He watched the man for a while and then went over to him and asked, "What are you doing here?" "I am praying," the man answered, "How are you praying, if you are not moving your lips?" Then this holy priest heard a wonderful answer: "I am looking at Him, and He is looking at me"!

The essence of prayer is – TO BE WITH GOD! Remember a time when both of you felt a great love for each other. Was it not enough to BE TOGETHER IN SILENCE – HEART NEXT TO HEART? Words, in a moment like this, would get in the way. This human, very deep experience of love can also become the way you experience prayer – in its very nature - the meeting of your human love with God, the source of very love.

Conclusion

1. God planned marriage as the union of a man and woman for a specific reason: to form a community of love, holiness, as well as, for procreation (having children).
2. Christ instilled a sacramental (sanctifying) dimension into marriage.
3. The Sacramental Marriage is a sign and a tool of God and His people in the community of the Church.
4. The Sacramental Marriage is a domestic church. In the words of Pope John Paul II, "the Church in miniature or the domestic church, the marriage and the family must be a school of faith and communal prayer." Only a family that is strong in its faith will overcome crises and becomes an evangelizing force in its environment, allowing the local community to experience the presence of God the Creator through them.
5. Engagement is a time of blessed preparation for the Sacrament of Marriage.

When, as an engaged couple, you decide you want a Sacramental Marriage, you are actually making a mutual decision to attain holiness together! YES, YOU ARE! Believe this. This is actually possible. However, to reach holiness you will have to make a great effort and have much patience and, most importantly, you will need grace from God.

Once you overcome the first difficulties on your road to holiness, do not give up believing in the reality of your success. Of course, sometimes it will be very difficult, because Satan will get in your way (just as he placed obstacles before me while writing this book), but with God's help you will overcomes every obstacle. Then, you will discover Jesus TOGETHER, enjoying His presence and grace in your lives. You will come to meet Him with growing joy as during Holy Mass, you offer Him the gifts of your engaged and sacramentally married life. You will become "rich" and with joy, you will share this Godly wealth with others.

Married couples have been canonized as saints in the Church. Others have died in an atmosphere of holiness. They made it. Try as well. I wish you success, though right now you may doubt that this is possible and you may be completely blind to any holiness in the near future of your life.

Entrust yourselves to the Holy Spirit, the Sanctifier, and ask Him to lead you and sanctify you! Present all your life plans to the Spirit of Love and Holiness! Do not be afraid. Entrust your whole married life to Him! Call often to Him: "Come Holy Spirit and fill us with your Love. Transform our married hearts!" Ask for the care and protection of Our Lady, the most holy, and St. Joseph, her beloved – the best and the holiest of patrons for married couples in human history.

Courage! Do not be afraid! Jesus is with you and wants to help you in the Sacrament of Marriage. He will send His Holy Spirit, so that – like the Apostles – He will lead you on the road to do the will of the Father until you are sanctified and in perfect union with the Heavenly Family.

A Moment of Reflection and Dialog

1. Recall the date of your Baptism and include it in your annual prayer calendar.
2. Prepare an annual calendar of prayer: when and for whom are your going to pray (include birthdays, Saint's days, weddings, Baptisms, First Communions, anniversaries as well as the beginning and end of the school year, and so on).
3. Start praying together; find prayers together during your engagement and marriage.
4. Start participating together and actively in the Holy Mass.
5. Come to Mass earlier, to pray and go to Confession (if you need to), so that you can participate more fully in the Eucharist; preparing for Confession takes time; you may need to do this at home.
6. Meet before Mass (as an engaged couple) to think about the intention you will offer and what to pray for (go during the week when possible, but be sure to go every Sunday).
7. After Mass, talk about the experience (do not be embarrassed to do this), later (when you are parents), discuss your experience with your children on the way home from church and at home (this will also help mobilize you all to participate in the Liturgy together).
8. Think about which Sacramentals were used in your families.
9. Do you use Sacramentals in your life: which ones and why?
10. Talk about which Sacramentals you would like to use in your marriage and family life.
11. Which of the Sacramentals would you like to teach your children to use?

E. Prayers for Various Occasions

1. Prayers for Engaged Couples

For the choice of a good fiancé

God, the Almighty Father.
Grant me the ability to first know myself and Your plan for me.
Permit me also, to get to know the person I love and Your plan
for him/her. Allow us to understand one another and Your
plan for us. Help us to realize whether You want us to be engaged to each other.

O Lord!
May the Holy Spirit help us to grasp Your Will for our
plans and Your desire in our hearts and minds: should we be
engaged? What should we do, as an engaged couple, to come to
know ourselves in You and Your will in our lives? Who lives
and reigns forever and ever. Amen.

For the choice of a good spouse

O most perfect Father!
We stand before the most important decision of our
lives. We want to receive the Sacrament of Marriage. TO-
GETHER, WE WANT TO EXPERIENCE our future. Today,
as the end of our engagement nears, we know each other better.
We want undertake this definitive and irreversible lifetime decision which will join us until death. We ask You, as we did before our engagement:

Send Your Holy Spirit into our hearts and minds. Reassure us that You desire our marriage. Reassure us that You want
us to live in a Sacramental Marriage. Sanctify us in it and enrich
us with children. Lead us and one day, our family, on the pilgrimage from this earth to the House of the Father. Who lives
and reigns forever and ever. Amen.

Before Confession

Jesus, full of Love and Mercy!

We want to receive the Sacrament of Reconciliation and Penance and reunite ourselves with God and His people. Before the priest, your servant, we will confess our sins. May your Holy Spirit help us to realize our sins and their malice. We know that Satan is our greatest enemy: our personal enemy and the enemy of our engagement. Through the sins we have committed we have become slaves of evil. Hear our confession, which is filled with true sorrow. Forgive us and grant us true freedom. Protect us from the temptations of Satan. Renew our souls so that they can better love You. Renew our love as an engaged couple. Teach us to choose that which joins us, and to avoid everything that distances us from You and each other as an engaged couple. We ask this of You, Who lives and reigns with God the Father in unity with the Holy Spirit, forever and ever. Amen.

On the day of receiving the Sacrament of Marriage

God, Creator filled with Love!

When you created human beings as man and woman, you called them to a life as husband and wife. Today we want to realize Your plan in our lives and enter into the Sacrament of Marriage. We want You to be with us through every moment of our married lives. During our engagement, we did not choose each other just to have a "good time", but we decided to BE WITH YOU AND IN YOU, TOGETHER as husband and wife until the end of our days.

We invite You to be present not only during our wedding ceremony in church, but also to on our joint pilgrimage through this earth. We believe that you will sanctify our everyday lives. Jesus full of loving mercy! We ask this of you, Who lives and reigns forever and ever. Amen.

2. Prayers for Married Couples

After Receiving the Sacrament of Marriage

God, full of Love!

From the depths of our hearts, we thank You for calling us to a life filled with divine and human love and intimacy, intimacy of body and soul within our Sacramental Marriage. We deeply believe that you have chosen us from among many men and women as the proper candidates to become a husband and a wife in a Sacramental Marriage.

Remain with us in every moment of our marriage. Send your Holy Spirit upon us to sanctify every moment of our marital union: all of our thoughts and words, our plans and their realization, the communion of our hearts, souls and bodies.

Enrich us with children for Your glory and deepen our love as a mother and a father. Guide us safely along this earth as pilgrims and lead us to Your House. We ask this through Christ our Lord. Amen.

Morning Prayer

Almighty God!

We thank You for this past night. You now give us a new day, so that together we can realize the gift of marriage in our home and in our work. Bless us and those with whom we will work today for Your glory and for the needs of all people. Help us to live according to Your Will. Help us to see You and serve You in every meeting with every person. Sanctify us and our work. We ask this through Christ our Lord. Amen.

Evening Prayer

God, Father of us all!

Thank You for this day that has passed. Thank You for all the people we met with whom we shared Your love. We thank you for all the good with which You enriched our lives as Sacramental spouses. We ask Your forgiveness for the opportunities we did not seize to love You and others more, as well as, one another. Forgive our lack of respect for You and others. Bless us throughout the coming night. Allow us to rest and renew our strength, so that tomorrow we can continue to realize Your plans in our lives. We ask this of You, Who lives and reigns forever and ever. Amen.

Before Work

God, Creator of man and the entire world!

We thank you for your gift of co-participation in the creative act of "subduing the earth". Thank You for our work, which gives us the opportunity to develop and sustain ourselves. Sanctify us and our efforts. Help us to do everything the best possible way, so that the fruit of our labor can serve the good of many people. May St. Joseph, the patron saint of working people, beg for us all the necessary graces from You, Who lives and reigns forever and ever. Amen.

Before Traveling

God of our fate!

You know our paths and the purpose of our lives on this earth. Bless us on this road, so that we may happily come to the end of our earthly journey, in order to stand at the gates of Your Heavenly Kingdom. May this journey be according to Your Will. Send your Angel to care for us. We ask this of you, Who lives and reigns forever and ever. Amen.

Before a Marital Discussion

God, One in the Trinity!

You unceasingly lead a "dialog" within the Most Holy Trinity. Today, as we begin our marital dialog, send us your Holy Spirit, so that He may participate in it and direct our thoughts, feelings and words. May these moments be filled with honesty and a true search for a careful decision, which will bring us even closer to one another in truth and love. May this dialog strengthen each of us within our sacramental marriage. We ask this of You, Who lives and reigns forever and ever. Amen.

Before Sunday Mass

God and Redeemer of the world!

After the entire week You invite us on this Lord's Day to a meeting filled with love and offering within a Community of Pilgrims. Help us to prepare ourselves, so that we can participate fully, with a pure soul and a heart filled with love, together with the Eucharistic Jesus in the Holy Spirit – in praising the Father.

We bring You the gift of an entire week of our married life and we gratefully place it on Your altar. We ask You to accept our gift, purify it and present it to God the Father.

May Your coming to us in Body and Blood renew and strengthen our married love for the entire coming week which You bestow upon us. We ask this of you, Who lives and reigns with God the Father in the unity of the Holy Spirit forever and ever.

Amen.

Before Confession for Spouses

Jesus, filled with Merciful Love!

In a moment we will stand before You and Your priest, to confess our sins. Thank You for the gift of the Sacrament of Reconciliation and Penance. Send your Holy Spirit to help us realize what a great evil sin is in our personal and married lives. We stand in the face of truth: we are weak and we are sinful.

From the bottom of our contrite hearts we call to You: Lord, have mercy on us! Lord, forgive us our sins. Breathe into us a new spirit and give us a heart filled with the love of God and others.

Protect us with your grace against Satan and his temptations. Give the priest, who will be listening to our confession, a spirit of discernment as to our sinfulness and our needs.

Bestow upon us Your forgiveness and Your peace. We ask this of You, Who lives and reigns with God the Father in unity with the Holy Spirit through all time forever and ever. Amen.

At the Beginning of the Liturgical Year
First Sunday of Advent

Marana tha – Come Lord!

The calling for you to come as the Savior resounded through the ages, from the moment Adam and Eve walked through the gates of Paradise, and will continue until Your Second Coming on the Last Day.

It is the Advent of mankind – a time when people wait for the coming of God – joyful and fulfilled. It is also the Advent of God – a time when God waits for the people to come back to Him – this time is much longer and sadder.

O Lord, you have waited and still wait to enter into our human interiors to sanctify us with your grace. We have waited and still wait for You to free us from the enslavement of sin and to make us Your Children.

We thank You for this new Year of Grace in the Liturgy of the Church, so that we may experience even more deeply the mystery of our Salvation. Teach us to more fully take advantage of Your gifts of grace in our married lives throughout this new Liturgical Year of the Church. We ask this of You, Who lives and reigns with God the Father in unity with the Holy Spirit through all ages forever and ever. Amen.

At the End of the Liturgical Year

On the Feast Day of Christ the King

Reign over us, Christ the King!

From the depths of our beings, enriched with Your gifts, throughout this Year of Grace that we have experienced in the Liturgy of the Church, we cry out: *TE DEUM* – WE PRAISE YOU LORD! With hearts filled with gratitude, we cry out with Mary: MY SOUL WORSHIPS THE LORD!

O yes, Jesus! You came to us through the Liturgy of the Church, to sanctify our Sacramental Marriage during this earthly pilgrimage. With our entire hearts, we thank YOU FOR BEING WITH US AND BEING IN US.

We are sorry that we did not always allow You to reign in our souls. Forgive us our moments of weakness and sin – moments when we turned away from You. Today, we want to call out: be with us, Lord and reign in our hearts, in our thoughts, in our emotions and in every moment of our lives on earth. Lead us to the Father's House, so that we can be with You always in the Heavenly Kingdom. We ask this of You, Who lives and reigns with God the Father in unity with the Holy Spirit throughout all the ages forever and ever. Amen.

During the Illness of Your Spouse

Jesus, Doctor of the body and the soul.

How painful is the illness of a husband or wife. Help my spouse through this illness. May this illness be an opportunity for us to grow closer to You and to each other as sacramental spouses. Bestow upon us the physical health of our bodies and sanctify our souls and give us the ability for even greater love. Through the Sacrament of the Sick, grant us the gift of accepting our illness and offering it to You, Who lives and reigns with God the Father in the unity of the Holy Spirit throughout all the ages forever and ever. Amen.

After the Death of your Spouse

God, the eternal Father!

My heart is filled with sorrow after the death of my wife (husband). Nobody can replace his (her) presence in my life and in my home. I thank You for the gift of our years together in Sacramental Marriage. Forgive the sins we committed against one another. Show us Your Mercy and grant my spouse a place in Your House! Grant me strength in the difficulties of my single life. Be with me throughout the remaining years of my life. I ask this of You, Who lives and reigns through all time forever and ever. Amen.

"Good Jesus and our Lord, grant him (her) eternal rest."

3. Prayers for Parents

For my own family

Father, the source of all life!

Thank You for the wonderful gift of motherhood and fatherhood granted to us through our children. Sanctify us and our new vocation as parents. Sanctify our children for the glory of God and for the good of others. May they grow in friendship with You and all people. May they fill themselves with Your Wisdom and Knowledge, which they will need to lead responsible lives on this earth. May they be a sign of Your love and ours as well. May we, together with them, realize Your plan for Salvation in our daily lives. We ask this of you, Who lives and reigns forever and ever. Amen.

A Mother's Prayer

Lord!

You gave me the gift of motherhood. I am now a mother and my husband is a father. Therefore, I am a participant in the work of creating of a new person. I gave him (her) my body, and You, "oh my Lord", gave him (her) a soul and so miraculously formed the child in my womb. What an incredible gift! You entrusted me with this new person, so that from this moment on I would take care for him (her) like none other – besides Yourself – on earth. I thank you Lord, who lives and reigns forever and ever. Amen.

Mary, most Wonderful Immaculate Mother – Mother of Jesus Christ, help me to live out my vocation, so that I can be a good woman, wife and mother.

Mary, Queen of Families, pray for us!

A Father's Prayer

Perfect Father!

I am now a father, and my wife is a mother! What a wonderful and responsible vocation. Thank You for confiding to me and entrusting me to be a father to this new person, who will need our mutual love and care. Who lives and reigns forever and ever. Amen.

St. Joseph, Caretaker of Jesus and Patron of Fathers!

God Himself entrusted you with the care of His only Son and Mary, His Immaculate Mother. Therefore I put myself and my family under your providential care and I ask for your intercession with God. Help me to fulfill my vocation, so that I may be a good man, husband and father. Help me to secure adequate living conditions for my wife and our children.

St Joseph, Patron of the Church, pray for us!

For the Children

God, Father of us all!

Thank You for the wonderful gift of new life, through which You have called us to responsible motherhood and fatherhood. Thanks to Your grace, we have passed the gift of mortal physical life to our children. You, however, have given them the gift of eternal spiritual life. Teach us how to raise them, so that they will grow, not only physically, but also, spiritually. May they be our children and even more so, may they be Yours. May they grow in grace with God and with others. May they bring glory to You and to us, the joy of their growth in You. Who lives and reigns forever and ever. Amen.

Before the Birth of Your Child

God, Father of all life!

The time of birth is near. Bless us with the happy delivery of our child. Strengthen the baby and mother during birth, so that no complications arise. Grant them health and the kind assistance of people. Support the medical staff with your grace. May this newborn baby be a special gift of Your Love and ours as parents for the Church and the world. We ask this of You, Who lives and reigns forever and ever. Amen.

Before the Baptism of our Child

Lord Jesus Christ!

Thanks to Your blessing we have a child – a gift of God and our marital love. This child has enriched our marriage and transformed us into a family. It is our desire for this child to be welcomed into the Family of God as well. Lord Jesus, give this child Your grace so it can fully become a Child of God and a member of the Church. Immerse this child into Your death and grant him (her) new life. Help us and the godparents take up and fulfill the necessary responsibilities to raise this child and fill him (her) with love for God and others. We ask this of You, Who lives and reigns with God the Father in unity with the Holy Spirit throughout all ages forever and ever. Amen.

At the Start of the School Year

Holy Spirit!

God created the human person and commended him to "subdue the earth". The surrounding world as well as the inner being of the human person is filled with mystery. The material and the spiritual world contain mysteries that can be unraveled and known. The gift of learning and thought helps us better to understand ourselves and the world.

Holy Spirit, as we begin this new school year, come into our hearts and help us (and our children) obtain the knowledge to grow in much needed wisdom, so that we may come to know and realize God's plan for us and others, and through this come to love God and others more. We ask this of You, Who lives and reigns with God the Father and His Son throughout all the ages forever and ever. Amen.

During the School Year

God, the giver of every life!

Thank You for the gift of our child. Give him (her) the ability to learn what is taught at school and to be guided through life by Your Wisdom. We ask this of You, Who lives and reigns forever and ever.

Mary, Seat of Wisdom!

Lead our child on the path of God's Wisdom, so that he (she) may know and love Jesus with his (her) whole heart and may be faithful to Him throughout his (her) entire life.

Oh, Mother and Queen! Oh, St. Joseph!

Help us to be good parents and to help our child with our prayers, the love of God and all people.

Holy Mary and St. Joseph, pray for us and for our child.

At the End of the School Year

Holy Spirit!

The school year is ending, but gaining knowledge is never ending. We thank You for all Your help given to us (and our children). We thank You for the gifts of memory and the ability to learn. We especially want to thank You for allowing us to know Your Holy Will better and to love You more. Teach us to share what we have learned with others, so that we can be grateful together for all the gifts You continually bestow upon us. We also want to especially thank You for the gift of Wisdom that helps us to better understand the world, events, ourselves and others. We thank You, Who lives and reigns with God the Father and His Son through all ages forever and ever. Amen.

Before our Child's First Confession

Jesus, full of Love and Mercy!

Help our child to know his (her) sins, which come forth from a lack of love for God and others. With sorrow, may he (she) confess all of them before the priest, Your servant. Forgive and help him (her) to live every day according to Your Commandments. We ask this of You, Who lives and reigns with God the Father in unity with the Holy Spirit through all of time forever and ever. Amen.

Before our Child's First Holy Communion

Jesus, full of Love!

Today, our child will participate completely in the Holy Mass and receive Your Body and Your Blood in Holy Communion. We thank You for this amazing gift in the life of our child. From now on, be the most beloved Guest in our child's heart and mind. May our child always be faithful to You and grateful for this greatest gift of life. Reign in our child always, Lord, Who lives and reigns with God the Father in unity with the Holy Spirit through all ages forever and ever. Amen.

Before our Child's Sacrament of Confirmation

Holy Spirit!

Today our child will receive from You the gift of wisdom, understanding, counsel, fortitude, knowledge, piety and a fear of the Lord. By practicing these gifts, our child will receive the fruits of the Holy Spirit: love, joy, peace, patience, kindness, goodness, faithfulness, gentleness and self control. May they help our child to realize God's plan of Salvation and the vocation that God has given him (her). We ask this of You, Who lives and reigns with God the Father and His Son forever and ever. Amen.

Before our Child's Wedding

God, the Almighty Father!

Today, in Church, our child will make his (her) wedding vows before You and receive the Sacrament of Marriage. May this new sacramental gift continue to sanctify the newlyweds. Be with them in every moment of their sacramentally married life. Help them to become one body and one spirit in You, Who lives and reigns forever and ever. Amen.

Mary and St. Joseph!

Intercede for our children, newly married in the sacrament, for the necessary graces of God, so that they may persist in faithful love and enjoy the blessing of children. May Jesus sanctify their everyday marital, and later family, lives.

St. Mary and St. Josef, pray for them!

Before our Child enters Religious Life

Jesus, Good Shepherd and Master!

You bestowed upon our child the vocation to exclusively serve the Lord. We thank You for this amazing gift offered to him (her) and our family. In gratitude, we give You our beloved child as a sign of our faith and love. Reign in his (her) heart and mind. May he (she) remain faithful to You for their entire life. May he (she), attain complete happiness and joy on this earth in You, as well as, in eternity. We ask this of You, Who lives and reigns with God the Father in the unity with the Holy Spirit through all the ages forever and ever. Amen.

Before our Son enters the Seminary

Lord Jesus, the Highest Priest!

You bestow upon our son the greatest of vocations that can be given to a person on this earth. You want him to follow You and become Your priest. Take him under Your priestly care. Help him in his learning and help him to grow in love for You during his philosophical and theological studies in the seminary. Mold his heart according to Your own Sacred Heart. May he always be grateful and responsible for Your gift – the priesthood of Christ. We ask this if You, Who lives and reigns with God the Father in the unity with the Holy Spirit through all the ages forever and ever. Amen.

Before our Son receives the Holy Orders

Lord Jesus, Eternal Priest!

After many years of formation and study, our son will receive the Sacrament of Holy Orders from the hands of the Bishop. We thank You with our whole hearts for this most beautiful gift that You have given to us, our family, as well as the Church and the entire world. May our son, as a priest, remain devoted, faithful and grateful to You with his whole heart. May he serve Your People with devotion and sacrifice wherever You decide to send him through the decision of his superiors. May he, in great holiness, celebrate all the Holy Sacraments, especially the Eucharist. May he, with great joy and gratitude, feed the People of God with Your Body and Blood, so that he does not cease on his journey to the House of the Father. May our son be a priest according to Your Sacred Heart. We ask this of You, Who lives and reigns with God the Father in unity with the Holy Spirit throughout all the ages forever and ever. Amen.

Before our Child takes Religious Vows

Jesus, Good Shepherd and Master!

You have given our child the gift of a vocation to religious life. We thank You for this with our whole hearts. Today, our child will be making their religious vows to You. Ensure, oh Lord, that our child remains faithful to You and the religious community, who has accepted him (her) and desires that he (she) serves God and His people together with them. Bless our child. Sanctify him (her) in fulfilling his (her) everyday obligations in the community. Fill our child's heart and mind with Your Wisdom and with a desire to live a more perfect life in faith, hope and love. We ask this of You, Who lives and reigns with God the Father in unity with the Holy Spirit through all of time forever and ever.
Amen.

During the Illness of a Child

Jesus, Doctor of the soul and body!

Every illness is a painful experience - physically, psychologically, emotionally and spiritually - not only for the one who is sick, but also for those who surround him (her). The illness of a child is an especially painful situation, for the child, as well as, for his (her) parents and family.

We beg you, Jesus, bestow health upon our ill child. Help us to keep our deep faith that what is happening in his (her) life is Your will. Give us hope for his (her) recovery. We ask this of You, Who lives and reigns with God the Father in Unity with the Holy Spirit through all the ages forever and ever. Amen.

After the Death of a Child

God, Eternal Father!

You bestowed upon us the joyful gift of a child. Today, with great sorrow, we say farewell on this earth. There are no words to describe the pain we feel. As a sacramentally married couple, we believe You are a God of Love and Mercy. Grant our child a new life that is filled with happiness within Your Eternal House. Remain with us in our great sorrow, so that in You we can see the purpose of this death and perceive our child's happiness with You, Who lives and reigns forever and ever. Amen.

"Good Jesus and our Lord, grant unto them eternal rest."

After the Death of a Mother

God, Eternal Father!

My mother has left this world. She was the one who gave me life, carried me under her heart, gave birth to me and raised me. Today, with a heart filled with gratitude for the life she gave me, but also filled with sorrow for her departure, I pray with faith, asking You to look upon her with merciful eyes, forgive her the sins she committed during her life and except her into Your Heavenly Kingdom. May her soul rest in Your Peace. Who lives and reigns forever and ever. Amen.

"Good Jesus and our Lord, grant unto her eternal rest."

After the Death of a Father

God, Eternal Father!

My father has departed this world. My father, who together with my mother, cared for my life, my education and my upbringing. Today, with a heart filled with gratitude for his fatherly care and also filled with sorrow, due to his departure, I ask You with faith, to look upon him with the eyes of mercy, forgive him the sins he committed during his life and accept him into the Your Eternal House in Heaven. May his soul rest in Your Peace. Who lives and reigns forever and ever. Amen.

"Good Jesus and our Lord, grant unto him eternal rest."

A Moment of Reflection and Dialog

1. I will try to obtain a *Holy Bible*, *Catechism of the Catholic Church* and a prayer book.
2. I will try to write a prayer for:

- myself
- my parents
- my fiancé
- my wife or husband
- the family of my parents
- my tutors and teachers
- the Pope, bishops and priests
- my friends and acquaintances
- health for the sick
- the deceased, for eternal happiness in heaven
- those who govern, for their wisdom and responsibility

F. The Liturgical Year at Home

Advent

Advent is a time of joyous hope-filled anticipation and preparation for the celebration of the birth of Jesus Christ in Bethlehem as the Promised Savior on the liturgical day of Christmas, as well as, for His Second Coming at the end of all time. Advent is also a daily experience of the coming of Christ in another person, in ordinary life, and especially during the liturgy of the Holy Mass.

During the liturgical time of Advent, it is good to place an Advent "decoration" in a visible spot in your home. You could, for example, make a sign that reads: MARANA THA – COME LORD, and below it place an empty manger in an Advent wreath with figures of Mary and St. Joseph nearby.

On Sunday, you could lead an Advent ceremony in your home: a short prayer (your own, one from the Sunday liturgy or a prayer book) recited by the husband and wife, as well as the children. You could sing Advent songs, or pray the Litany to Mary, Mother of God.

It is also worth getting an Advent wreath and four candles (three purple and one pink for the third Sunday of Advent), but always take great care when around small children due to the fire risk. The Advent candles should be lit at the beginning of the prayer and extinguished immediately following it.

Also useful in celebrating Advent at home, is a "roratka" - a candle (decorated with ribbons, flowers or boughs of evergreens), which symbolizes Mary waiting for her Son, Jesus Christ. When we light this candle during individual or joint prayer, it reminds us that Mary is with us and that together, we wait for the coming of the Savior. She supports all of our good intentions and efforts, our prayers and preparations for a joyful Christmas. Our prayers and thoughts should often call upon her during this time of waiting and preparation. She, the Mother, will definitely plead for us with her Son for whatever graces we need. During this time of waiting, children may place red paper hearts - representing their good deeds - into the empty manger where later, baby Jesus will be placed on Christmas Eve. Let us cry out together with Mary - Come Lord, we are waiting!

Christmas Eve (Wigilia)

Before Christmas Eve, try to get some straw, a manger, and a figure of the baby Jesus. Place the manger on the dining room table or beside it. Put some straw inside the manger and cover it with a small piece of white cloth. With the lights turned low and the Christmas tree lit, the wife (mother) should bring in the little figure of baby Jesus, singing a Christmas carol, and place it in the manger. The husband (father) should then read about the birth of Jesus in Bethlehem from the *Gospel of St. Luke* and then finish with a short prayer. In accordance with the Polish custom, the head of the household, holding the blessed (by the priest, if possible) Christmas wafer (*oplatek*) in his hand, offers his best wishes first to his wife, then his children, parents and others who are present. Then, he shares the *oplatek* by breaking it with those present in the same order. Everyone present first shares their *oplatek* with the head of the household, who leads the prayer, and then breaks the *oplatek* with everyone else, while wishing each other loving blessings. Afterwards, everyone sits down at the table and the Christmas Eve meal begins. On this night, discussions that divide or are critical of others are inappropriate and should be avoided. Christmas Eve is a time of unity and love. For the person holding the *oplatek*, it should be a sign of his reconciliation with God and others. After completing the Christmas Eve meal, the participants should sing Christmas carols (it is important to have the words available to all who need them). Before singing carols about the shepherds, you could bring in their figures and place them by the manger.

NOTE: participants should not drink alcohol (leave it for another occasion), especially if they are going to Holy Midnight Mass afterwards!

Christmas Season

Christmas Day, as well as the Sunday after Christmas, are days of the celebration of the Holy Family (from Nazareth). This is a special time of unity, joy and gratitude towards God and people. During Christmas, it would be good to thank God for the birth of Jesus in Bethlehem and the Holy Sacraments. During the feast of the Holy Family, you should give thanks for the gift of the Sacrament of Marriage and for each child that enriches your lives with the gift of motherhood and fatherhood. This day should be celebrated at home, together. Reserve time to share your personal feelings with one another: spouses, parents and children. It is worth preparing (especially the first time) a text of vows or renewing your wedding vows and family vows: parents toward their children, children toward their parents and children to each other.

In the Polish tradition, the Christmas season is a time during which the parish priest visits his parishioners. Such a visit to their homes will entail prayer, a blessing of the home and conversations that strengthen the marriage and family, as well as, their ties to the parish community. Prepare the table for this visit by covering it with a white tablecloth, and placing candles, a cross, holy water and an aspergillum on it. If may also place the blessed wafer (*oplatek*) on the table. The letters "K+M+B" written over your front door with blessed chalk on the feast of the Three Kings will be a reminder of the long and difficult journey the wise men undertook to find Jesus and Mary; their offering of gifts and that "they departed for their own country by another way." These words should remind the household members about their mission in today's world: finding Jesus and sharing Him with all the people they meet in their lives. After meeting with Jesus, a person comes away "different" – transformed – as he returns to his family and home.

Lent

This is a very difficult time in the lives of Catholics. It brings to mind the suffering of Jesus because of the sins of the people and therefore, our own sins. Suffering is part of human life. Marriage and family are not free from sin and suffering. Lent is a time to reflect upon the suffering of Jesus in His historical Passion, which is relived in every person to this day, in order to help us. This is a difficult, but blessed time of inner change, becoming a better person by breaking with evil habits and doing good with the help of God's grace. This is a time of looking for God's grace through the Sacrament of Reconciliation and Penance, as well as, in the Eucharist. It is a time of participating in community prayer and Lenten retreats. During Lent is it good to bring the Crucifix into a prominent place in the house with words such as written next to it: FORGIVE US LORD or THANK YOU LORD. During this time, the Church suggests that its faithful pray the *Stations of the Cross* (at least on

Fridays), and pray, for example, the *Lenten Lamentations* ("*Gorzkie Zale*" - a Polish traditional devotion usually sung on Sundays). In order to fully experience this time of Lent, and to enter into the mystery of the Passion of our Savior and His Love, you should take up these types of prayers. You may join in the meditations of the Passion of Christ in your parish or at home. When we immerse ourselves in these reflections, prayers, practices of Lent and the Passion of Christ, we give God a chance to change our hearts and minds.

It is worth freeing your home from the noise of loud music, movies or arguments. Silence helps to create a Lenten atmosphere and helps renew relations between spouses and family members. Weekly meetings with the members of the family during this time to discuss issues in the marriage and family may be planned. Participation by the entire family in an examination of conscience and receiving the Sacrament of Reconciliation and Penance is a good idea.

Easter Season

ALLELUIA! THE LORD LIVES! This call is fundamental to our faith. It refers not only to the historical resurrection, but also to today's reality. This truth empowers our day to day life. Jesus, who died and was resurrected, lives in the reality of married and family life. The contemplated past becomes the liturgy of the present. Yesterday becomes Today!

It is good to participate in the Triduum Sacrum (the three Holy Days: Holy Thursday, Good Friday and Holy Saturday) in order to truly experience the deepest truths of our Christian faith.

Holy Thursday is the day when the Sacrament of the Holy Eucharist and the Sacrament of Holy Orders were established. This day should be a great day of thanksgiving to Jesus for these Sacraments and for His presence in the Eucharist, the Living Love and Food of the Faith, as well as, for priestly, married and family love.

Good Friday is the day of the death of Jesus Christ, Who died so that we could have life and we could live for God. This is a day of complete silence in the home (no music, radio or television), of contemplating the suffering and death of God, who became Man, our Brother, Savior and Friend. During Good Friday, we should feel the pain of our sins.

Holy Saturday is a day of prayerful meditation and waiting, so that the death of Jesus on the Cross may be fruitful in our married and family lives. This is a day of grave tranquility in the house. It reminds us of the historical uncertainty about Jesus: "but we expected..." as well as today's uncertainty regarding the deaths of our loved ones: "are they saved"?

And finally, the day of greatest joy in the Church year: EASTER – THE DAY OF THE RESURRECTION OF OUR LORD! THE LORD LIVES! Every Sunday is a "mini Easter". The echo and reality of the joyful "Alleluia" resounds in the Liturgy of the Church thorough out the year, except during the period of Lent.

For these joyous days of Easter, decorate the Cross of Christ, who defeated Satan, sin and death. Only in Him can we be victorious over evil in our hearts. It is a good idea to have a sign that reads "ALLELUJA" to remind us of this special and singular event in the history of time: the RESURRECTION OF JESUS!

The Sunday after Easter is the Feast of Divine Mercy, which most perfectly reminds us of that Jesus' Heart is filled with Merciful Love and opens to every person who asks for it, as well as, the necessity of mercy in the life of every person, including sacramentally married spouses and their families. It would be appropriate to pray the *Chaplet of Divine Mercy* together on this day. This prayer is an expression of our adoration of God in the mystery of His Mercy in everyday married and family life. It would be even better if praying the Divine Mercy Chaplet became a daily occurrence in the family or at least on every Friday - a way to continuously call for Mercy for ourselves and the whole world. On this day, you can also participate in the

3:00 pm prayer of the Divine Mercy Chaplet at your parish, if it is available.

Pentecost

This celebration reminds us of the promise fulfilled by Jesus to the Apostles at the Last Supper and the revelation of the Church to the whole world. It is also a day of calling to Jesus to send this same Spirit into the hearts of modern world couples, families, friends, acquaintances, and others, so that He may change the face of the earth. Pope John Paul II, on June 2, 1979, finished his first homily at Victory Square in Warsaw with this great outcry: "May Your Holy Spirit Come and renew the face of the earth, this earth!" Wow! And how God responded to this outcry and answered it: in 1980, "Solidarity" was organized; the government declared Martial Law on December 13, 1981, and Poland was freed from the oppression of Soviet Communism in 1989. Then, the system of terror that oppressed millions of people fell in the rest of Eastern Europe. A revolution of minds and hearts ensued, without a revolution filled with blood and death. Oh, how powerful is the action of the Holy Spirit.

How very necessary He is for spouses, in order to sanctify their human lives, especially their married and family lives. This celebration should renew the gifts that spouses and their children received through the Sacrament of Confirmation. Before this feast day it would be worth preparing and hanging a banner in your house that reads: MAY YOUR HOLY SPIRIT COME AND RENEW US!

Jesus - Savior and King

The Father loved the world so very much, that He gave us His only Son, so that we would believe, and through our faith, we would have Eternal Life. Jesus is the Word Incarnate, the Son of God and the Son of Mary the Immaculate Mother. It was Jesus who changed the marriage of Joseph and Mary into that of the Holy Family in Nazareth. Jesus, without their knowledge, as twelve year old boy, stayed back in Jerusalem. When Mary and Joseph found Him, after looking for three days, in the Temple, Mary questioned Him. She asked: *Son, why have you done this to us?* (Lk 2:48). He enlightened them by responding that he was where He belonged - indeed he should be here, taking care of his "Father's matters."

His awareness of belonging and being in unity with the Father: *the Father and I are one* (Jn 10:30) was constantly before him. He came to fulfill the will of the Father and by being *obedient to death, even death on the cross* (Phil 2:8). Jesus Christ unified us with the Father through His death on the cross at Golgotha. It is because He loved the Father and He loves us that He not only died and was raised, but He also remained with us, within the Holy Sacraments, especially the Eucharist.

After the Resurrection, Jesus appeared many times and reassured all those who saw Him about His Love for us. He also appeared throughout the history of the Church to remind us of His great Love for all people; to remind us of His Heart filled with Love (as seen by St. Margaret Mary of Alacoque), open to every person; about His great Mercy (as seen by St. Faustina Kowalska), which burns Him like a fire, since He wants to pour it out to poor sinners, giving them His grace of forgiveness and sanctification.

June is dedicated to the Sacred Hear of Jesus, in order to "kindle" the human heart with God's Love. The June Liturgy is, in a special way, necessary for spouses, who in the presence of Jesus and the Church, vowing their mutual love until death. Why are there so many difficulties in fulfilling these marriage vows? Could it be that after they leave the Church they leave Jesus behind instead of inviting Him into their homes and hearts?

It is worth returning to Jesus, the source of all sacramentally married love, in order to regain God's Love and your love toward one another throughout your lives. It is worth warming your heart with Jesus's Love and kindling your own love towards Him. It is only when Jesus lives in the hearts of both sacramental spouses every day, that He strengthens them and helps them to deepen and renew their love. May the *Litany to the Sacred Heart of Jesus* in June and on First Fridays of the month become a fervent call to greater love in your sacramental marriage.

May Jesus reign in your hearts and help you to share His Love with one another, with your children and all the people who come your way throughout your lives. It would be good, for example, to make a banner and hang it in an appropriate place in your home (in June) that reads: "HEART OF JESUS - REIGN IN US", or to display a picture of the Sacred Heart of Jesus.

Mary - Mother and Queen

God entrusted His only Son to Mary, the Immaculate Mother. Consider this: maybe we should also entrust our marriage and family to Her?

In the history of the Church, such devotion has lead to great holiness. Pope John Paul II offered himself completely and irrevocably to Mary: TOTUS TUUS - ALL YOURS. When he was shot on May 13, 1981, and was being rushed to the Gemelli clinic, he cried out: "Mother, rescue me!" She did, and on the first anniversary of the shooting, he flew to Fatima, Portugal to thank Her personally in the sanctuary that is dedicated to Her. What a wonderful pontificate. He served Jesus through Mary as John Paul II, the Great, the Pilgrim Pope, Pope of God's Mercy, Servant of Mary, a Pope who unified leaders of other religions and nations, believers and non-believers throughout his life, and someone who gave lessons on suffering and dying until he reached his deathbed, and afterwards at his funeral in St. Peter's Square in Rome.

The Church dedicates many days to Mary throughout the liturgical year, as well as, two whole months: May, for prayers imitating pilgrims on their way to Loretto (the Litany of Loretto); and October – for praying the "Our Father" and "Hail Mary" and supplemented by biblical meditation on Jesus and Mary in the twenty mysteries of the Holy Rosary.

It would be worthwhile to find time - especially on Saturdays, to individually as well as jointly thank Mary for Her unending intercession to Jesus for us. It would be a good to ask Her for all the necessary graces needed for sacramentally married spouses and their families. Devotion to the Mother of God is not only needed for wives and mothers in order to deepen their spirituality of marriage and family, but it is also important for husbands and fathers to learn a deeper respect and love for their wives and mothers, as well as, responsibility for the presence of God and Mary in one's personal married and family life. It is worth making a banner with the words: "MARY, OUR MOTHER AND OUR QUEEN!" and hanging her picture in an appropriate place in your home during May and October.

St. Joseph - Bridegroom and Patron

The Gospels do not tell us much about St. Joseph, since they are meant to tell us the story of Jesus, who was born in order to save us. Yet these few references to St. Joseph are filled with dramatic events.

First, he experiences an enormous test in Nazareth in regards to the conception of Jesus. He did not understand what had happened. Being *a righteous man* (Mt 1:19), he wanted to send Mary away quietly. In those times the Law was brutal (she could have been condemned to death). Only after such a noble gesture on his part "to put her away discreetly", God intervened and enlightened him. With this enlightenment, St. Joseph lived until his death.

The second dramatic event came about because *there was no room for them in the inn* (Lk 2:7), so that Jesus could be born - in human terms - with dignity. There was only a simple roof over the heads of Mother and Child at the moment of birth.

The next dramatic event refers to the words of old Simeon at the temple, that this Child would be *a sign that will be contradicted*, while to Mary, Joseph's spouse, Simeon said, *"and you yourself a sword will pierce"*, (Lk 2:34-35).

The following difficulty was the dramatic flight of Joseph, Mary and the baby into Egypt, an enemy country, where they settled until they were called back home (Mt 2:13-15).

Then another problem arose: Joseph could not return to Bethlehem, the place of Jesus' birth. Therefore, he returned to Nazareth and lived there in great silence (Mt 2:19-23).

The final dramatic event referring to St. Joseph, as recorded by the evangelists, was the three day long search for the "lost" twelve-year-old Jesus. When they finally found Him in the Temple and were relieved that He was alright, He surprised them with His words, which were not a justification for his absence, but rather almost incomprehensible words about His Father (Lk 2:41-48).

St. Joseph, while observing Jesus grow up, never revealed the truth about his role as His guardian, but not father. There, in Jerusalem, the words of Jesus reminded him of who He was and His awareness of it. It was, in fact, this quiet husband and guardian (though regarded as father) who showed great marital maturity and responsibility. There is nothing unusual about the fact that the Church has declared St. Joseph as its Patron. Personally, I believe he also deserves the title of Patron of Sacramental Marriages. The two special days assigned to him during the liturgical year in the Church are March 19, where we honor him as the Bridegroom of Our Lady, and the May 1, where we honor him as a Worker, and the Patron of working people.

May Wednesday become the day of pray to him as the intercessor of the necessary graces needed for sacramentally married couples, especially for husbands and fathers. It is worth making a banner which reads: "ST. JOSEPH, OUR PATRON" and placing it in an appropriate place, or we can hang a picture of his image.

A Moment of Reflection and Dialog

1. Together, develop a "liturgical calendar" for your home.
2. Include all of your own yearly celebrations in your "domestic liturgical calendar".
3. Think about how to honor Mary and Joseph in your marriage and family?
4. Discuss how you would like to celebrate the liturgical periods in your "domestic Church"?
5. Decorate your home during the special days of your "domestic liturgy".

VI. Being a Family Person

1. God's Plan for Us

Then God said: *Let us make human beings in our image, after our likeness. (....) God created mankind in his image; in the image of God he created them; male and female he created them* (Gen 1:26-27). *It is not good for the man to be alone. I will make a helper suited to him* (Gen 2:18). When God, the Creator, created human beings in His image, He planned them to be part of a family! God is a communion of Three Persons: the Father and Son and Holy Spirit.

The Son of God became man and was born of the Virgin Mary, and thus He transformed the marriage of Joseph and Mary into a Holy Family. Living within a marriage and family of believers and who practice their faith - taking advantage of the Holy Sacraments - is a wonderful way to prepare for life in the world. This kind of atmosphere helps the husband and wife, and father and mother, to acquire suitable experiences they can pass on to their own beloved children. Parents, who lead a life with God, are able to create a God-filled environment in their day to day family lives. In such an environment, the couple will joyfully await and long for the gift of a child, to whom they will be able to communicate their love of God and people. This much desired child is seen and accepted as a gift of God and their own human love: a gift from God and their mutual gift as a husband (father) and a wife (mother). The child opens a new world for them, and they open to the child a house filled with God's love and their parental love.

In John Paul II's *Letter to the Families*, he writes: "Among these many paths, the family is the first and the most important. It is a path common to all, yet one which is particular, unique and unrepeatable, just as every individual is unrepeatable; it is a path from which man cannot withdraw. Indeed, a person normally comes into the world within a family, and can be said to owe to the family the very fact of his existing as an individual." (nr. 2).

2. The Family Person

The family is the fundamental unit of society as substantiated by natural law. This is a bond of blood and fate within a common home. A family is an institution that has a common goal, as well as, a hierarchy of rules and responsibilities. A family is a union in which each person is loved and loves. This kind of family is a reflection of the Family of God in Three Persons through:

a) its Trinitarian makeup – a father, mother and child;
b) its calling and power to procreate;
c) the love of the father, mother and child.

A family person:
- is someone who creates an atmosphere of mutual love within the marriage, which encompasses each of the family members at all times;
- loves every member of his family more than he loves himself;
- is concerned about every member of his family;
- is always available to everyone in the family;
- most importantly, lives with God and always shares Him with his family members;
- must first ensure that God is known and loved by everyone in the family – the parents as well as children!

It is only then that the family will be strong with God! Children who come from such families will desire to establish their own families and lead lives similar to the ones that they experienced with their own families - families, which they had come into as the long desired gifts of caring parents and a loving God.

Is this possible? Why not? In the history of the Church, we know of such marriages and families, like Joachim, Anne and their child Mary, or the Holy Family itself, or the family of St. Teresa of the Child Jesus of Lisieux. In such families, God was always what was most important. In such families, the spouses and parents lived with God every day. The experience of the Sacrament of Marriage lived out in everyday life is the best preparation for one's own family life. It is also a source of God's grace for every member of the family.

The celebration of Holy Eucharist by the entire family is a source of irreplaceable supernatural help. John Paul II, in *Familiaris consortio,* writes: "...the Eucharist is a fountain of charity. In the Eucharistic gift of charity the Christian family finds the foundation and soul of its 'communion' and its 'mission': by partaking in the Eucharistic bread, the different members of the Christian family become one body, which reveals and shares in the wider unity of the Church. Their sharing in the Body of Christ that is 'given up' and in His Blood that is 'shed' becomes a never-ending source of missionary and apostolic dynamism for the Christian family" (nr. 57).

3. Building Marriage and Family Traditions

Remember to honor all the good, existing traditions of both families. These traditions have a great meaning in a person's life. Good, long family traditions have positively shaped the lives of many saints and generations of people. During your engagement, consider selecting and merging the valuable traditions of both sides into your new family. Rejecting them by one side would be a sign of disrespect for the other family and will become an unnecessary cause of conflicts. You must remember that family traditions are sanctified by customs that sometimes reach back many generations, even hundreds of years. Then, they are even dearer to a family. It is not necessary to destroy the past, but rather, it is important to jointly select from all these traditions, those which are most valuable and to include them in your new marriage. These traditions should then be enriched with your own new marriage and family practices. The traditions should be passed down to your children with proper explanations and the respect that they deserve. A person without tradition is a person without "roots". Of course, it is understood that these traditions should not break down your marriage and family, but rather, enhance them. You also have the right to build your own traditions as well. However, remember that religious family traditions are especially important. They were shaped in the hearts of many previous generations of believers and lovers of God. This is one of the important reasons **a Catholic should marry a Catholic**.

During your engagement, it is necessary to get to know the traditions of both families. In these traditions you can find the answer to this question: Who are the people in this family I am entering into and what are they like? Very often, traditions make an impression on the way one thinks and how he or she was raised in a given family. As I have mentioned earlier, it is very important to especially learn the religious traditions. They are a part of the interior religious life of a family and the members who grew up in it. Be aware also of destructive traditions: broken families, multiple divorces, crime, alcoholism, gossiping, arguing, verbal abuse, long bouts of unemployment, a neglected home, and so on. You cannot immediately heal these families or the children of these families who may become your candidate for a spouse. I have met exceptions to this; however, it cost both parties many sacrifices and demanded constant attention in order not to fall back into the "ugly spirit of the past".

During your engagement, take into consideration how to incorporate good traditions into your future marriage. There should be plenty of time during the engagement to discuss these things and how to creatively adapt the traditions of both families for the benefit of your spouse and future relatives. Then, "family" visits will not be an unpleasant responsibility or disastrous surprise, but rather more of a joyful meeting filled with genuine interest in the lives of those closest to us. You should always inform your spouse ahead of time and prepare him or her for visits with your family.

Visits to each other's families should not stop after the wedding, especially not for trivial reasons. Misunderstandings should be resolved through dialog. A husband from a family with which there is conflict, should stand by his spouse during conversations, if she is not at fault. If she is obviously wrong, she should admit to it and apologize. It is very difficult to visit the parents of a spouse who only accept their own child, but not their daughter-in-law or the son-in-law. Sometimes, after many failed attempts to convince your parents - you will have to side with your spouse. The Sacrament of Marriage demands that you place your spouse first, your children second, the rest of your family afterwards, and so on. You cannot turn your back on your husband or wife in an attempt to impress someone else (even your parents or friends). This kind of love for your parents or this kind of friendship is deceitful and sooner or later will destroy your marriage.

Parents should cultivate positive relationships between their children and the grandparents of both sides. Frequent visits will help you children get to know and love their grandparents. This "second motherhood and fatherhood" that your parents will experience as grandparents, is often more beautiful than their first experience as parents. Your children will quickly notice whether or not you show respect for your own parents. Through their observation of your positive example, they will learn gratitude and will imitate you in your respect for their grandparents.

4. Finances - The Marriage and Family Budget

Every marriage has a specific income and expenditures. In many countries, governments allow for deficits in their budgets. This is because politicians do not pay for policies with their own money, but rather, take money from the pockets of taxpayers by increasing taxes. This is not a model to emulate in a marriage or a family. The budget of a married couple and their family, very often, requires much sacrifice and financial discipline from both spouses and all members of the household. There was a time in the United States when you could see the sons of wealthy millionaires working and pumping gas at gasoline stations during their summer break! Their parents taught them respect for work and money, even though they had so much of it. It is always easiest to spend someone else's money!

Fundamentally, income is fixed and so are certain expenses. Of course, unexpected situations may arise which will cause "headaches" and quickly deplete your pockets, your purses, wallets and even your bank accounts. That is why it is necessary to prepare a budget for your home on an annual, monthly and, if needed, a weekly basis. A marital or family budget should categorize its expenses in order of priority: *necessary, useful,* and finally, *for pleasure.* It is also a good idea to put away a certain amount for unforeseen (*necessary* or *useful*) costs that may arise.

There should be no favoritism in the budget, nor should it be stingy toward anyone. A wonderful example is the first community of early Christians in Jerusalem, where each person received according his or her needs. It should be the same within a marriage and family. Of course, necessary expenditures must be budgeted realistically, meaning they have to be based on the actual incomes of both spouses. The budget should be prepared by both spouses and when the children are old enough, they should participate in the process as well. Preparing a budget teaches everyone financial responsibility. The amount of income as well as and a list of priority expenses should be clearly stated. It is absolutely unacceptable for one of the spouses to hide income from the other. However, certain restrictions should be placed on bank accounts to prevent one spouse from going bankrupt if his spouse robs him and takes off. Unfortunately, situations occur in various marriages, even the sacramental ones. Foresight is necessary. It is not a matter of mistrust, but rather of a transparent future, so that unnecessary pain may be avoided.

Adult children, who are financially independent but are still living at home, should contribute an agreed upon portion of their income to the household budget for shared expenses. This is not "payment" to the parents, but rather, "financial solidarity and responsibility," as well as, fairness in the family. Parents should not be terrorized by the words: "I'll move out!" Such a child does not love his parents and is definitely not grateful to them or the rest of family. Permissiveness of the parents in this sphere will not teach their children financial responsibility in the present or in their future marriage, family or social life.

A husband or wife who has a tendency to overspend should only have access to an agreed upon, reasonable amount of money. Turning a blind eye on the financial missteps of such a person is, in fact, participating and encouraging the further deformation of their character and supporting an injustice to the rest of the family. A husband should understand that a wife's (woman's) expenses are different than his own and overall, are usually greater than his (a man's). However, the spending of either side should not be excessive. Bigger expenses should be agreed upon by both the husband and wife. Children should also be taught financial responsibility. They can receive a set allowance in order to learn to budget for necessary expenses, but they should never be paid for work in the house or for school work.

A budget should include support to your parish as a *necessary* expense (in American conditions, this could be about 2.5 percent of total income or one hour of income), as well as, any other money given to known charities, or to help friends in unforeseen and emergency situations (note: it is possible to lose friends by lending them money). It is good to involve children in the decision about how much money to offer to the parish or charitable causes; especially the children who work, so that they may also decide to give an offering to God through their parish. Such a lesson on budgeting within the home will open their hearts and minds to the needs of others, and helps them to be sensitive to the financial situation of their own family and local parish. The budget itself is a private family matter and for many reasons (jealousy, gossip, possible theft, etc.) should not be discussed with others.

A Moment of Reflection and Dialog

1. Individually, prepare a list of actual expenses: necessary, useful, and for pleasure.
2. Mutually, as an engaged couple, prepare a similar list, covering the expenses connected with your wedding; as a married couple, prepare a list of marital expensed; as parents, prepare a list of family expenses.
3. Together, prepare a realistic, positive marriage and family budget (income and expenses based upon the actual expenses of married and family life).
4. Discuss how you should protect yourselves from bankruptcy which due to overspending (watch for the excessive spending your fiancé; after the wedding, when more money is available, there will also be more opportunities to spend it and to be dishonest about it). Start to think about what kind of husband or wife and how many kids can you afford! Surely there will be a cost, but how high will it be and how will you be able to afford it?

Now pretend you are economists. Start by establishing your total income. Agree upon your expense categories:

1 - Necessary
2 - Useful
3 - Pleasure

First separately, then jointly, make one list from the two:

	His	Hers	Children
Food, drinks	___	___	___
Clothing, shoes	___	___	___
Cosmetics, hygiene	___	___	___

Entertainment (movies, parties, lottery, hobbies)

    —   —   —

Family vacations   —   —   —

Books, music   —   —   —

Continuing education   —   —   —

Religious education   —   —   —

Career training   —   —   —

Education of children   —   —   —

TV, radio, computer   —   —   —

Presents/gifts   —   —   —

Pocket money (each according to their need)

    —   —   —

Furniture, appliances   —   —   —

Home repairs, remodeling   —   —   —

Loan, credit card payments   —   —   —

Children   —   —   —

Necessary help in the home   —   —   —

Purchase of a house   —   —   —

Purchase of a car   —   —   —

Restaurants, coffee shops   __   __   __

Sporting events, fitness clubs   __   __   __

Offering for mass intention, (weekly, monthly)

                                 __   __   __

Donations to parish, charity   __   __   __

Savings (for unexpected expenses)   __   __   __

Savings (for retirement)   __   __   __

Insurance (house, health, car)   __   __   __

Planned expenses (weddings, baptism and Holy Communions)

                                 __   __   __

Bank savings (which accounts, interest, bank fees)

                                 __   __   __

Other expenses:_____   __   __   __

      _____   __   __   __

Now take note of the final number:

Income: _____

Expenses: _____

Difference: _____

Congratulations on completing this exercise of preparing a budget for your life together. Soon, this will no longer be a game and the realities of life will set in. You will create an actual weekly, monthly and yearly budget and you will even plan for your retirement. Mistakes may cost you dearly. Financial problems have led many not only to financial ruin, but also emotional disaster, and even to the breakup of their marriage and family. May your financial balance always be in the "green," meaning, may it be positive. God Bless!

VII. Help for Hurt Spouses

Even with the best intentions, people often get hurt, even in Sacramental Marriages. The reason is simple and obvious: spouses are also... sinners. The Sacrament of Marriage does not protect you completely from sin, not even the ones we commit against ourselves. Furthermore, Satan often attacks those people who try to live with God each day, even more so than others. It is as if, when they sin, Satan backs off for a moment, since he has achieved his goal: to halt the development of intimacy and separate these people from God. When St. Paul lamented to Jesus over his inner struggles with sin, he heard these words from Him: *My grace is sufficient for you, for power is made perfect in weakness* (2 Cor 12:9). God may allow for temptation to reach you as spouses, but He will also give the necessary grace to overcome them.

1. Negative Solutions

a) The most common and seemingly easiest (though negative) solution is separation, which often leads to the permanent breakup of a Sacramental Marriage. It is true that the Catholic Church allows for temporary separation so that the spouses may think over and pray through the causes of their difficulties, or so that they may, for example, participate in counseling or meetings for married couples experiencing a temporary crisis. The longer problem is "pushed under the rug", however, the harder it will be to resolve. A lack of faith in the ability to overcome a crisis is based on the futile efforts to change by one person and his or her broken promises. As spouses who experience difficulties, yet possess a living faith, you will search for positive solutions that will be good for both of you. Go to your parish priest or other competent and believing person (marriage counselor) for help. It is never too late to positively resolve a crisis.

b) Another negative, sinful and nowadays common "solution" is divorce. It is a great tragedy for the spouses, and even more so for the children, who for the rest of their lives will be marked with the "stigma of a broken family". The Church does not accept nor acknowledge divorce, though is sympathetic and understands the contributing factors. A person who is divorced may partake in the Sacraments for as long as he or she lives alone or with his or her children. Of course, during Confession, that person should always state that he or she is divorced, especially if much of the fault lies with him or her.

Statistics in the USA are disastrous: over fifty percent of marriages (not necessarily sacramental) end in divorce within the first seven years. Eighty percent of divorced persons enter into new, non-sacramental relationships (half of them within 3 years of the divorce). Every year, over a million children suffer from the painful effects of these divorces. The main problem that leads to divorce is a lack of communication between spouses (according to a survey taken by marriage therapists), next, are the loss of common interests, loneliness, lack of sexual compatibility, unfaithfulness, loss of attraction of the marriage, conflicts due to children, violence, problems with in-laws and financial difficulties ("Christopher News Notes", April/May 2000).

c) An effort to resolve a marital crisis by seeking an Annulment of the Sacrament (this is not a "church divorce", but rather a proclamation that the Sacrament in effect, did not take place) is a lengthy process. It is not expensive, and contrary to popular opinion, the sum required by the local church court does not influence the final decision. There is no guarantee that the outcome will be positive, because the Marriage Tribunal may not find any impediments to the marriage and declare that a Sacrament had taken place. In this situation, neither side may enter into a new marriage. A negative decision shows the futility of trying to force the Church into solving marital problems in this way. This is, therefore, a negative solution, just as the two that were listed above.

2. Positive Solutions

a) Search for a resolution together in a spirit of mutual love. This requires both sides to admit their own personal faults, as well as your spouse's, no matter how small. This positive method leads to an earlier recognition of a problem in one's own marriage and in consequence, the joint participation in various sessions, marital retreats, or meetings with marriage specialists, as often as it takes, to resolve the problem. This method demands honesty and openness, as well as, a mutual search for the common good in your marriage.

b) Prepare for Holy Reconciliation together. This "session of honesty," first at home, later in the church, will increase your awareness of the need for Christ's presence and for each other's forgiveness first, and then forgiveness you will receive from Him. Preparing for Holy Confession together will often prevent marriage problems from growing. Many sacramentally married couples can bear witness to this fact. Financially, this is the least expensive method, though internally it bears a high cost, since it requires that you admit to hurting another person, your lack of love, and the need for you to change for the better and actually bring these changes into your everyday married life.

c) The most valuable solution is to pray together as a couple every day at home, to ask for God's help, then go to Holy Mass together and together receive Jesus in Holy Communion. This model is the best preventative measure for marital problems, and when a crisis develops, it will help to overcome it.

d) A community of faith and prayer, like a parish or a prayer group, helps troubled marriages tremendously. The knowledge that there are people who pray for and ask for God's graces for them, should help both spouses feel that they are not alone in their troubles. Anniversary celebrations of the Sacrament of Marriage, retreats or days of recollection (within the parish or sponsored by the parish) for sacramentally married couples, renews them spiritually and helps them to see themselves and their marriage problems in a positive light.

A Moment of Reflection and Dialog

1. Think about whether you have any emotional wounds from before your Sacramental Marriage and search for an explanation and justification for them.
2. Were you healed of these wounds before your marriage?
3. Have you been hurt during your marriage thus far? How many times and how long did it last?
4. Have you tried to talk about these hurtful situations?
5. Did you listen to one another carefully and apologize for any pain you might have caused?
6. Has the person responsible for causing pain to the other made up for what he or she did and change for the better?
7. Have you forgiven each other?
8. Have you asked God for forgiveness together?
9. Did you search for a positive solution together? Did you find it?

Sometimes, regardless of your effort, it is impossible to change right away. Then, time and patience is needed from both spouses. Maybe you ask yourself this question: do I have the physical, psychological and spiritual strength to continue being hurt by my spouse? I know you do not deserve any more wounds. Try to offer to God, for the intention of the conversion of your spouse, your prayers, a Holy Mass, and also your pain. Pray individually as well as together, asking God for help. Invite your children, even the little ones, to pray (though you do not need to explain everything to them). Seek professional help.

St. Monica begged the Lord for 18 years. Her husband and son converted! Have courage!

VIII. Selected Issues

A. Impediments to Marrying in the Catholic Church

Not everyone (even Catholics) may enter into the Sacrament of Marriage. The Code of Cannon Law (CCL, 1983; Pallottinum 1984) provides the following general principle: "All can contract marriage who are not prohibited by law" (Can. 1058). Before announcing your intended marriage in the church, make sure there are no obstacles that would prevent or delay you (for example, special permission, or a Dispensation to Marry) from entering into the Sacrament of Marriage.

1. Diriment Impediments

The Code of Canon Law (1073) states that "a diriment impediment renders a person incapable of validly contracting a marriage", and then continues (1083-1094) to list these impediments as: a lack of appropriate age, impotence (infertility), previous marriage, different religions, holy vows, a public vow of celibacy, abduction, wrongdoing (murder or conspiracy to commit murder of a spouse in order marry), blood relationships that are either legal and natural. Anyone who tries to enter into a marriage with impediments and without receiving a dispensation from the appropriate Catholic Church authority does so invalidly. "Only the supreme authority in the Church can authentically declare when the divine law prohibits or invalidates a marriage" (Can. 1075.1). Canon 1078.1 explains: "the local Ordinary can dispense his own subjects wherever they are residing, and all who are actually present in his territory, from all impediments of ecclesiastical law, except for those whose dispensation is reserved to the Apostolic." The Church does not have the authority to give a dispensation from impediments arising from God's Law (natural and thus stated). Therefore, a dispensation may not be given for impediments of family blood connections in a direct line or in the second degree of the collateral line (Can. 1078.3, 1091), an existing marriage bond (Can. 1085) and impotence (Can. 1084). On the other hand, dispensations may be granted (for an important reason) for impediments of human law (Church law), in order to help a person achieve a greater good.

2. Defects of Intellect and Will

The section of the Code of Canon Law that deals with marital consent lists intellectual ability and will of the parties as necessary to enter into a valid Sacrament of Marriage (Can. 1095-1103), including:

a. sufficient use of reason;
b. proper judgment concerning matrimonial rights and obligations;
c. the psychological capability to assume the essential obligations of marriage (psychological tests are recommended);
d. both sides should know that marriage is a permanent partnership between a man and a woman ordered to the procreation of children through sexual cooperation;
e. knowledge of the person and their essential qualities;
f. a conscious choice, not brought about by force or coercion.

Serious deficiencies in these areas, in either one or both sides that trying to enter into a sacramental marriage, cause the invalidity of the sacrament. Canon 1107 states: "Even if a marriage has been entered into invalidly by reason of an impediment or defect of form, the consent given is presumed to persist until its withdrawal has been established."

3. Lack of Canonical Form

Marriage is a Sacrament and a public legal act within the Catholic Church. Therefore, it is important to maintain the appropriate canonical form, as stated in the Code of Canon Law: "Only those marriages are valid which are contracted in the presence of the local Ordinary or parish priest or of the priest or deacon delegated by either of them, who, in the presence of two witnesses, assists, in accordance however with the rules set out in the following canons, and without prejudice to the exceptions mentioned in Canon 144, 1112.1, 1116 and 1127.2-3." (Can. 1108.1)

I realize that this information is a bit general and may only serve to signal a possible problem. I quoted specific texts from the Code of Canon Law. You may read them yourselves or go to a parish office, where the local pastor should be able to help you to better understand the official interpretation of these and other Canon Laws of the Catholic Church.

It will do no harm to ensure there is no impediment which prohibits you from being joined in a Sacramental Marriage. My advice: do not become engaged to someone who you know is not free to enter into a Sacramental Marriage. The initial joy from a civil union often, especially in church, transforms into an increasing pain that comes with not able to receive the Holy Sacraments. I have seen many people suffer like this, and I have suffered along with them.

B. Practical Advice before Marriage

1. At the Parish Office and Necessary Documents

Specific regulations vary from country to country and diocese to diocese. Parishes may have their own ways of handling the details pertaining to the Sacrament of Marriage. Please be open to dialog. When filling out necessary documents, always be sincere and honest.

A Few Useful, Practical Points:

a. Catholics, who wish to enter into a Sacramental Marriage for the first time, should bring the following documents to the parish office: a "new" copy of their baptismal certificate (issued within the past six months - check local requirements) and your confirmation certificate (basically required).

b. Catholics, who have been married previously in a civil ceremony, non-Catholic Church, a sect, and so on, should first go to their parish office and obtain specific information for their given situation. It is not a good idea to pick a date for the wedding, since it is unknown if and when the Catholic Church authorities will give permission for a Sacramental Marriage.

c. Catholics, (who are not widows or widowers), who have entered into a previous Sacramental Marriage, must present a decree from the Marriage Tribunal, which declared the previous union invalid from the start. This process can often be lengthy and depends on many different factors. However, it is worth pursuing a Declaration of Nullity, if the Catholic has *justified* doubts regarding the validity of their previous sacramental marriage. I remember the great joy of many couples, who, after many years of living together, were encouraged by me to fill out and file the necessary papers, and finally received a declaration from the Catholic Church authority that their previous marriages were in fact invalid. What joy indeed, when these people were able to receive the Sacrament of Reconciliation and Penance, followed by the Sacrament of Marriage! You can imagine how wonderful they felt when they received absolution, and then during the Holy Mass, they received the Sacrament of Marriage as well as Jesus in Holy Communion. They were and continue to be very grateful. Yet, a feeling of regret remained in them for not taking care of this important matter earlier.

d. The Catholic Church may grant special permission for a Catholic to enter into a union with a non-Catholic in a Catholic Church or beyond it. When such permission is granted, the Catholic may continue to receive the Holy Sacraments. See your local parish for more detailed information.

Personally, I would like to warn Catholics about the difficulties that will arise sooner or later in such unions - especially with people who are Muslims or Jews and with persons from certain Protestant communities (who are very anti-Catholic), or members of sects. In such unions, Catholics must often bear ridicule of their Catholic faith by their non-Catholic spouse, and in many cases they (mostly women) are pressured into abandoning their Catholic religious practices.

The inability to practice one's religion often leads to a loss of faith. A common problem is that children are prevented from being Baptized and are not allowed to be brought up in the Catholic tradition (this is a very painful situation and the Catholic spouse feels betrayed because, before the marriage, the non-Catholic spouse officially agreed to the Catholic upbringing of any children - this was a prerequisite for obtaining permission to marry).

I recommend caution when traveling (even for family visits) with your husband and children to Muslim countries (there it is common practice to take away a wife's passport to prevent her from returning back home). Trusting such a husband, even one who was raised in a democratic, western culture, can turn to tragedy (there are many examples of this women and mothers who have had to escape from Arabic countries, and some have even been turned into films). Of course, things could be different, but there always remains a risk. During Pope Benedict's stay in Turkey, Polish married woman from mixed marriages were interviewed about their situation and rights. It appeared the husband practiced Islam and the wife her Catholic faith. There was no mention, however, of the children and whether or not they were Baptized or how they are being brought up.

Again, there may be exceptions, but who will give you a guarantee? Moreover, practicing your faith alone isolates and alienates you, regardless of your love for your spouse.

2. Selecting a Date

Only after you have arranged all the necessary documents, should you choose a date and time to celebrate your Sacrament of Marriage. Book the hall for your wedding *only after* you have established a date (usually with the priest) at your parish office. This has nothing to do with the whims of the priest, but rather, the objective conditions that may permit, delay or in some cases even forbid your sacramental marriage from taking place at a particular date or time (required documents, conflicts, etc.). Making stiff demands, especially at a large parish, may only make matters worse.

Save yourselves and the priest in the parish office from unnecessary and unpleasant discussions by having an open mind. Who knows, this may be the priest who performs you wedding ceremony, so behave in a way that will keep all of you from feeling uncomfortable later. Surely you want the celebration of your Sacrament of Marriage to be a great, joyous and unforgettable occasion starting your journey together as a married couple. Keep a joyful, sunny spirit that will spill over into your new life together. Perhaps you will need the services of this priest again someday? Life is full of surprises.

3. Preparing for the Celebration of the Sacrament of Marriage

The priest at the parish office should not only determine the date of the ceremony with you, but also discuss the following matters:

a) Details for the Church Ceremony
- Scripture Readings;
- The Prayer of the Faithful;
- Participation in the liturgy through reading and singing psalms;
- Music (usually in collaboration with the parish organist);
- Decoration of the church (flowers);
- Wedding rehearsal details (this custom is unknown in Poland, while in the US and Canada it is a necessity and one that often takes too long) - the couple must inform the participants of proper solemn behavior in the church and the need to show full respect for Jesus in the tabernacle (avoid unnecessary discussions inside the church);
- "Style" of entering or exiting the church:
  - in Poland, the couple enters the church together, followed by the bridal party;
  - in the US and Canada, the groomsmen lead the guests to their seats, escorting the parents of the bride and groom to their pews last. Then, they go to stand with the groom and the best man who are already waiting at the altar. The bridesmaids wait at the entrance to the church and walk in ceremoniously to meet with the groomsmen at the altar. Small children follow, carrying the wedding rings on a pillow. The maid of honor comes next, and finally, the bride is led down the aisle by her father, who then hands her over to the groom. After the Holy Mass, the newlyweds exit

first, followed by the entire wedding party, the parents and finally the guests;

o Mixed style – the bridesmaids walk in with the groomsmen, and the father of the bride escorts his daughter to the altar, handing her over to the groom. After the Holy Mass, the newlyweds exit first, followed by the bridal party, children, parents and the rest of the guests.

The celebration of the Holy Mass and the Sacrament of Marriage is what is most important, not the style in which it takes place, though the artistry of the celebration enriches the experience.

b) Donation Amount - The diocese may have an established donation amount (call the parish office). It is important to take note of sum in your wedding budget. Remember, this is not a "payment" for receiving the sacrament, but rather your participation in parish life, an invitation of the parish community to share your joy. If you are having a very small, modest wedding, the priest will understand that you are more intent on the celebration of your sacrament than the wedding reception and may suggest a proportionally smaller donation than if you were planning a large-scale, grand reception.

c) Photography, filming videos – It is important to inform the professionals about the parish rules regarding photography and filming during and after the Holy Mass. Remember that the priest is the main celebrant and the celebration of the Sacrament of Marriage – your wedding – is not a Hollywood movie production. Some parishes do not allow filming during the Holy Mass or have their own photographers or specially installed equipment within the church (there churches like this in the Archdiocese of Detroit) so that what is most important is not lost: the celebration of the Sacrament of Marriage, with the presence of Jesus at the threshold of the newlyweds' lives.

4. Celebrating the Sacrament of Marriage

The celebration of the Sacrament of Marriage may take place during Holy Mass (when both participants are Catholics and are able to take communion) or without the celebration of Holy Mass (often when there is a mixed marriage).

a) Before going to the Church:

- Go to confession a couple days before the ceremony or the morning of to receive the Sacrament of Marriage in a state of grace (have time for prayer and silent reflection before the wedding);
- Before leaving your house, ask your parents for their blessing for your new life;
- Arrive at the church early (out of respect for the people gathered there - the bride is very important, but not the most important, though on this day she may be the most beautiful, not only for her groom).

b) At the church:

- Remember that Christ and the two of you are the most important (not the photographs and film);
- Give yourselves to God and one another through the sacramental vows of love and faithfulness till death, and remain open to new life;
- Pray along with everyone else during the Holy Mass;
- During the Prayer of the Faithful, add a prayer for your parents (provide this text of this prayer to the priest before the Holy Mass);
- During the Offering, offer yourselves and your love to Jesus;
- After receiving Jesus in Holy Communion, thank Him for the sacrament and ask Him to always remain in your hearts;

- With Jesus in your hearts, ask Him, Mary and St Joseph, to care for you as spouses.

c) After the Holy Mass:

- Take a moment to pray (kneeling or standing);
- Thank God for the mystery of your love and for His sacramental blessing;
- Invite the most wonderful and noble of guests to your wedding celebration and into your new lives (as in the Gospel): Jesus and Mary (as at the wedding in Cana), as well as St. Joseph.

5. Celebrating the Sacramental Marriage - the Wedding Reception

It is important to remember that when you leave the church, your sacramental life as a married couple does not end but rather, begins its presence in the world around you. The sacramentally married couple should *never* leave Jesus and His Mother behind in the church, but rather, invite them to the wedding reception, as they were present at the wedding feast in Cana. The sacramentally married couple will always need Christ and Mary.

The wedding reception should never become a "festival of alcohol and drunkenness." For this reason, among others, you should carefully consider which guests to invite. There people who will not come to the church celebration, but will go to the reception just to have fun, eat well and drink their fill. Of course, all of your the guests should be present in the church to pray with and for the newly wedded couple. Those people known for their drinking problems should not be invited to the reception to avoid problems and brawls.

On the July 27, 1969, I presided over the wedding of my schoolmate, Marian, and his wife Maria in Kudowa Zdroj, Poland. Before the ceremony, I told him I would remain at their wedding reception as long as I did not see any drunkenness. I went away for a moment to say my Breviary prayers before midnight, but up until then, except for the wedding toast, there was no alcohol on the tables. I did not see a single intoxicated person. Maybe in another room, some alcohol was present. The atmosphere was excellent, however, and it lasted late into the night.

Of course, people may drink at weddings; even Jesus turned water into wine at the wedding in Cana. Jesus changed the water into wine because they had run out. Yet, it is important to demonstrate self control and dignity. The wedding reception should not lead the people paying for it, namely the parents, to bankruptcy. This is a delicate matter. Since your parents are paying, they also have a right to make decisions. They should, however, take your opinions into account because, ultimately, it is your wedding. There will always be someone who finds something to criticize. Maybe you can eliminate this by... not sending that person an invitation. The wedding should be filled with people who are happy for you and your parents. Sometimes, in the case of divorced parents, you may have to make a difficult and painful decision: to invite or not to invite them, and if yes, under what conditions. In most cases, you should invite both of them, so that they may be there to bless their child. Before making such difficult decisions, it is worth praying to the Holy Spirit for guidance.

C. Living Arrangements

Not all couples are lucky enough to live in their own house or apartment after their wedding. Sometimes, it takes a long time before they can have their own place. This is not conducive to developing their marital bond. Conflicts arise. Something always seems to be off. Living under someone else's roof, even if it is your parents' house, takes a toll. It is important to show the young couple a great deal of tact and allow them to have their own freedom to build their own identity and gain their own experience.

When it comes to living together, certain important matters should be discussed right after the wedding. Your parents should not have to support you. "Saving money" is a wonderful thing, but may also come back to hurt you and cause a lot of damage, like an Australian boomerang. You, as a married couple, should ask your parents about the costs of sharing the living space. If they do not want to suggest an amount, then you should propose a sum and pay it every month. It is also good to organize your living space to fit your tastes; however, this is a delicate matter and requires the home owner's permission.

Do not be afraid or ashamed to hang a cross and perhaps a picture of Mary in your living space or at least in your bedroom and later in your children's rooms. It would be good to meet in front of these Holy signs every day and pray. Sometimes you may need a lot of joint prayer! There is an English proverb that states: **Who prays together, stays together**. This is a great truth of life. Praying together has saved many marriages, even those in great crisis. When we stop praying together as a couple, we gradually drift away from God, our spouse, and our family, which may later lead to separation and divorce. These are very painful situations, experiences and consequences for the rest of your life. Do not be ashamed to be known as practicing Catholics in the place that you live.

> Once, Fr. Jozef Kaminski, TChr, told me about a visit to the home of one of his parishioners in Goleniow, Poland, which occurred after Christmas: "The house was very nice and beautifully decorated. I began to look around, and the lady of the house noticed and said, 'Father, you are looking for a crucifix. Just a minute, I will get one'. She opened the bottom drawer of a cabinet and among all the junk she had stashed in there, she pulled out a little cross. I took the cross in my hand and said, in front of her: 'Oh, Lord Jesus, you surely don't fit in here'."

I myself have visited thousands of Catholic families in their homes. It is always very painful to see when, in the grandest rooms, there is no trace of Catholicism, or when in the rooms of children, who attend church, or even serve at Holy Mass and sing in the choir, there are many posters on the walls, but no cross or holy picture – or if there is, it is very small or barely noticeable.

May Jesus on the Cross have the most prominent place in our homes. Let us remember His promise: *"Everyone who acknowledges me before others I will acknowledge before my heavenly Father* (Mt 10:32).

IX. What next?

This is a fundamental question you should ask yourselves before entering into the Sacrament of Marriage. The goal of your engagement is not the church wedding, just as the point of seminary studies is not ordination. Actually, it is the opposite; the years of engagement and seminary are only the preparation for a wonderful married or priestly life. Married life begins after your ceremonial marriage vows are made before God in the presence of the priest and others gathered inside the church. The newly married couple should not "rest on their laurels" after the wedding, but rather, should continue to develop their Sacramental Married lives!

The great gift of the Sacrament of Marriage presents a great challenge to the spouses: TO ALWAYS BE TOGETHER WITH JESUS UNTIL DEATH! Do not be afraid, Christ will offer you his never ending assistance. He will never leave you. Trust in Him, even during your most painful situations. He will be your friend. This is His sacrament for you. He is Present in it, for you, at every moment.

In marriage, one side should never take advantage of the goodness and hard work of other side. The open dialog of the engagement should continue as open dialog in the marriage of the same two people! It should never resemble this Polish saying: "when they marry, they change". If there is a change, may it be for the better, otherwise the husband or wife will feel deceived. This is a horrible feeling, especially for the woman, or wife.

It is clear that the responsibilities of married life at home as well as beyond it must be divided. From now on, both spouses are responsible for their married life and later, when children arrive, for their family life. There is no room for intimidation or blackmail in a marriage. It is wrong to say: "You're my husband now, so you have to do this" or "Since you are a wife, do the work a woman should do!" Marriage cannot be slavery! One does not marry in order to force his or her spouse to do anything. One marries in order to share the difficulties and joys of his or her entire married and family life.

The Love that joins two people in the Sacrament of Marriage, will itself direct loving and responsible spouses towards the duties in their everyday lives. This is obvious, but only then, when there is authentic love between the two spouses. Married life is not a harem or a work camp. Therefore it is essential to discuss and decide on many fundamental issues before marriage, so that are no unpleasant surprises afterwards.

Once a reporter asked a beautiful, newly married wife in Hollywood: "Your husband says you spend too much money, is this true"? "Yes," she answered, "He wanted a beautiful wife and it'll cost him!"

Once in Chicago, a woman asked me to help her to get a well know lawyer to take her case. I did not know either her or him. She gave me the phone number to his office. I called and his secretary informed me that he was unavailable because he was in court. I asked to her leave a message for me. I also, jokingly, asked the secretary to ask her boss what kind of wife he has: dear, dearer, or the dearest. I had to explain that by "dear", I meant "costly." I heard the secretary's laughter. She called me back the next day and informed me that the lawyer would take on the woman's case because he liked my little joke. She added that her boss laughed and said his wife is definitely the dearest (most expensive)!

Do you know the difference between an adult and a child, when it comes to toys (hobbies)? Adult toys are more expensive! A man, who has an expensive, beloved hobby, will probably not give it up and will continue to spend a great deal of money on it. He forgets, however, that after the wedding, his situation has changed dramatically: all of the money he earns is now shared, not only his. This situation also applies to the wife, who may have loved to spend enormous amounts of money on jewelry, perfume, clothes or travel, before marriage. Now she must remember that the money she is spending is shared, even if she earns it.

After your Sacramental Marriage, a very important test of your authentic motives will be the way you practice your Catholic faith and participate in the Holy Sacraments. A conversation like this between spouses will not do: "Get dressed; it's time to go to church." "If you want to go to church, go by yourself and pray for me. I don't feel like going today. Besides, I have work to do at home. Go already, and leave me alone." At this moment, should you not challenge your spouse by responding: "I went to church alone before marriage and we were married so that we could PRAY TOGETHER AT HOME AND AT CHURCH. I am not yet a widow or divorced!"?

How much pain can be found in hearts of wives, who must go to church alone, especially when they see other married couples participating in Holy Mass together! Remember, the first compromise in marriage drags with it a whole series of other ones.... How long can a person live like this? Where is the honesty and fairness, the true marital love? Living in a constant state of compromise will never be living in love, but rather, in never ending stress and submission. This kind of life leads to a greater and greater frustration, which may be hidden inside at first, but after awhile, may explode with consequences difficult to foresee. Love joins two people in all things, especially in their meeting with God, who is Love and the source of all martial love.

I once heard an incredibly beautiful example during a grand reception celebrating a couple's golden wedding anniversary. When forced to say a few word, the wife said only one sentence: "My husband, in 50 years of marriage, has never offended me, not even with one word."!!!! She had a very good memory. Tears appeared in the eyes of many of the women and wives. The guests rose to their feet and rewarded the couple with clapping and cheers. What glorious testimony of this couple's 50 years of married love and life! This is what I wish for you with all my heart.

A Moment of Reflection and Dialog

1. Prepare for the celebration of your wedding anniversary every year.
2. Discuss the good and bad experiences from the previous year.
3. Apologize to one another for any wrong you may have done to your spouse.
4. Reserve a mass intention to be celebrated for you to thank God and one another for all the good you have done for each other in the last year.
5. Think about what you can do to change for the better.
6. Celebration your wedding anniversary at home or by going out.

Final Reflections

These short reflections demonstrate how important and how intellectually and emotionally demanding the decision is of choosing your fiancé, the person, who will be your future husband or wife, who practices their Catholic faithfully and will later be committed to a life in Sacramental Marriage. This is the vision that I would like to propose to the young, engaged people reading this book. To those of you who are already married, I would like to say that it is never too late for Christ, who is present in your Sacrament of Marriage, to send His Holy Spirit to you to sanctify you. Pray to God for the gift of holiness in your engagement and marriage, and I will also ask for this gift to be given to you, by God in the Holy Trinity and through Mary, Mother of God and Her Holy husband Joseph.

To be human is a great gift, but it is also an enormous endeavor for the person himself and his surrounding community. It is worth being a person who continually develops himself and becomes increasingly noble in his love for God and other people.

It is worth being a fiancé who is dedicated to getting to know himself as well as his beloved fiancée, in order to establish a new sacramental life together lasting until death. It is worth being a sacramentally married spouse who, by the Will of God, and not only that of humans, will enrich your lives and will become enriched by the life of his spouse. BEING together requires an enormous amount of work on yourself and also, a great collaboration with God and the other person.

The gift of being human requires the discovery of God's DNA hidden within your soul: His image. Your engagement and sacramental marriage require openness to God and your beloved spouse. God is the One who unites one person with another. The way we love other people is a gauge which demonstrates our love for God. St. John, the Apostle, warns us against a feigned (false) love toward God. He writes that *whoever does not love a brother, whom he has seen cannot love God whom he has not seen* (1 Jn 4:20). St. James connects love to faith: *...faith without works is dead* (Jas 2:26).

It is worth considering the mystery of God's presence in ourselves, in our engagements and marriages, in order to notice the abundance of gifts received from God through and within other people. God, in His generosity, has endowed women and men with the gifts that they need to reach their full potential within their engagement and marriage: the gifts of personal and mutual dialog, sexuality, sacredness, parenthood and family, which infuses and renews marriage. These gifts are also callings. The human is an imperfect being and needs constant development at every stage of his life. The mutual gifts of a husband and wife make them more sensitive to one another and develop their marital dialog, while the gift of children takes them on a new path of life as parent pilgrims on their way to the House of the Father. What a fantastic calling: to love and be responsible for your marriage and family, for your own as well as your family's salvation.

Thank you for your enduring patience, which has allowed you to reach the final pages of this book of reflections. Every chapter and its selected topics require further reflection and contemplation. There are and will be more popular and educational reading materials on this subject. During the pontificate of John Paul II, Institutes for Family and Marriage in his name were established in many countries. Research and teaching on these matters is conducted there. In writing these priestly reflections, from "my heart to yours", I wanted to help, even if just a little. I would also like to invite those people who have greater knowledge and more experience in this area, as well as a talent for writing, to prepare more practical books (such as guide books) for those who are engaged or married.

Congratulations on the sacramental journey you have chosen together into the unknown through your engagement, marriage and finally, family. Congratulations also to those, who are spouses, mutually support each other in their journey over this hard land toward the House of the Father. I admire those of you, who are parents building a family strong with God, who unites with one another during your daily meetings with God and in God. These meetings with God should always renew your unity and married sacramental love.

Every human journey should begin with God, remain with God and realize His Plan to lead you to the House of the Father. Eternal life with God in the House of the Father should be the ultimate goal of every person and even more so of sacramentally married spouses. All other goals, though important and wonderful, should be considered in the light of the ultimate goal of the human person: the salvation of the souls of the husband and wife. The goal of the Sacrament of Marriage is holiness because, "nothing that is unholy will enter into the Kingdom of Heaven".

The goal of marriage is neither the couple nor their children. None of their – even most spectacular – accomplishments on this earth are its goal. All marital goals should lead the sacramental couple to be with God on earth, and later in heaven. Therefore, whatever you accomplish on this earth, always look to the end result: will it lead to your salvation as an engaged or married couple, and as parents, as well as the salvation of your children and other people? To achieve this, you will need to BE FRIENDS TO ONE ANOTHER IN GOD IN YOUR EVERYDAY LIVES!

Your friendship cannot be based on a false love, on hurting each other, or ignoring each other's mistakes. If you are married, it cannot be purely spiritual without sensuality. Your friendship will therefore be a "blend" of the spiritual and physical, which encompasses your spiritual and sexual love, your virtues and your weaknesses. However, every true friendship has to be connected to the greatest friend, Jesus Christ.

In the *Book of Ben Sira* in the Old Testament, we read: *"Faithful friends are a sturdy shelter; whoever finds one finds a treasure. Faithful friends are beyond price, and no amount can balance their worth. Faithful friends are life-saving; those who fear God will find them."* (Sir

6:14-16). In another Old Testament verse in Ecclesiastes (Qoheleth), we read: *"Two are better than one....if the one falls, the other will help the fallen one."* (Eccl 4:9-10). St Paul says that women in marriage want to please their husbands first, and similarly, the husbands want to please their wives (1 Cor 7:33-34). Of course, because married couples should go to God TOGETHER, not individually! I wish you this kind of success: holiness; and at the end of the pilgrimage of your sacramental marriage, that you reach the House of the Father. Your friendship in God will help you to attain happiness on earth and in heaven. I wish you, from the bottom of my priestly heart, the kind of friendship that will help you reach happiness and holiness.

The vocations of marriage and priesthood are so important and essential to the Church and to the world, as well as filled with such difficulty and responsibilities, that Christ Our Lord gives those who have decided to follow and fulfill this call, the help and blessing of two Sacraments: the Sacrament of Marriage and the Sacrament of Priesthood. One needs the other, and both need Jesus to fully realize their vocation. The Priest serves sacramentally married couples and the whole of the People of God as a steward of the Holy Sacraments. The married couple accepts services of this gift and enriches it with their prayers and holiness. They also increase the members of the Church, from whom God chooses many for marriage and some for priesthood. Christ is the ultimate purpose of life for the married, as well as, for priests. Furthermore, Christ is the source of all the authentic love, joy and happiness of all the Children of God, who walk the ways of their vocation according to God's Plan.

For those of you who would like to deepen the effectiveness of this reflection, pray for others, who – like you – have already read or will read them from beginning to end, and who will try to live according to the principles of God and the Catholic Church, which is the guardian and teacher of His ways.

Remember me in your prayers, and those who supported me with their words and prayer while this book was written.

Thank God for the gifts He gave me during my work. Please also pray for those who reviewed it in the name of the Catholic Church and gave me their positive support. I promise you, I will pray for you. May we one day meet TOGETHER, in the House of the Father, as God's Family.

May Jesus, Mary and St. Joseph lead all of us as a Family of God's pilgrims to the Kingdom of Heaven. May the Holy Spirit sanctify every moment of our pilgrimage.

The founder of the Society of Christ, Cardinal August Hlond, wrote these memorable words in the Guest Book at our World Headquarters in Poznan, Poland: "Between us there is no distance." May these words help us to remember each other in our prayers.

Upon completing this part of the book, which was filled with the reflections of a priest/pastor and someone who is a friend to you, may we deeply and with gratitude, consider the St. Paul's words about love in his first letter to the Corinthians. We are all called to love on this earth and even more so afterwards when this pilgrimage leads us to the House of the Father, to eternal life filled with the Love of God.

Hymn of Love

If I speak in human and angelic tongues
but do not have love,
I am a resounding gong or a clashing cymbal.
And if I have the gift of prophecy and comprehend
all mysteries and all knowledge;
if I have all faith so as to move mountains but do not have love,
I am nothing.
If I give away everything I own, and if I hand my body over
so that I may boast but do not have love, I gain nothing.
Love is patient,
love is kind.
It is not jealous,
[love] is not pompous,
it is not inflated,

it is not rude,
it does not seek its own interests,
it is not quick tempered,
it does not brood over injury,
 it does not rejoice over wrongdoing
but rejoices with the truth.
It bears all things,
believes all things,
hopes all things,
endures all things.
Love never fails.
If there are prophecies, they will be brought to nothing;
if tongues, they will cease;
if knowledge, it will be brought to nothing.
For we know partially and we prophesy partially;
but when the perfect comes,
the partial will pass away.
When I was a child, I used to talk as a child,
think like a child, reason like a child;
when I became a man,
I put aside childish things.
At present we see indistinctly, as in a mirror,
but then face to face.
At present I know partially;
then I shall know fully , as I am fully known.
So faith, hope, love remain, these three;
but the greatest of these is love.

(1 Cor 13:1-13, NABRE 2011)

Statements of Sacramentally Married Couples

The following statements were gathered through a questionnaire I prepared and distributed to pastors in several parishes in the US and Canada. I also sent it to some sacramentally married couples I know in Poland and Canada. In the US and Canada, the questionnaire was inserted into the parish's Sunday bulletins at the following locations: Holy Trinity in Chicago, IL; Maximilian Kolbe in Milwaukee, WI; Our Lady of Czestochowa in Sterling Heights, MI; St. Brother Albert Chmielowski in San Jose, CA; Sacred Heart in Guelph, ON and Our Lady Queen of Poland in Toronto, ON.

On February 2, 2007, I began to add the questionnaire responses to this book, which essentially had already been completed. I did this on purpose so that my reflection would not be influenced by the responses. I formulated the questions so that they would be general yet in line with the various chapters of this book. This way, responding couples were able to provide their own very personal reflections. I hoped these statements would supplement and enrich this book with the authentic experiences of sacramentally married couples.

I thought I would have difficulty selecting from the statements. However, it was not too hard, since only a few respondents returned their filled-out questionnaires on time. For some, the questionnaire may have been a bit difficult, since it required deep thought. I left the decision on how to introduce the questionnaire to each parish priest. Some were inserted without explanation or sometimes, encouragement was given to couples to respond. I am very grateful to those couples who did respond and shared their experiences. I believe they will help the readers, especially engaged and newly wedded sacramental married couples.

I quote the literal responses of the participants. Some of the responses were shortened (due to difficulty in reading some of the handwriting) and certain grammatical mistakes corrected.

Several responses needed to be translated. The names of the respondents are given at the end of their statements.

Preparing for Marriage (Within Your Family)

I grew up in a "broken" family. My parents divorced when I was just a little girl. Nevertheless, my mother was an amazing example of a wife and mother. She was the role model that has stayed with me to this day.

Otylia (married 26 years)

The best family "guidebook" is our parents. Observing them, we later expect a similar relationship with our spouse.

Teresa and Jozef (married 12 years)

We learned how to be good spouses from our parents. In every marriage, there are joyful, sad and difficult moments. Our parents, through their example, taught us how to celebrate the joyful moments, how to help each other in difficult times and how to work together to overcome obstacles. In these times, when the word "marriage", unfortunately, has less and less meaning, it is very important to teach our children true values and the real meaning of the word "marriage".

Ryszard and Joanna (married 15 years)

I have always seen my parents and grandparents working, practicing asceticism and praying. They were a rather wealthy family. They loved their land as they loved themselves. They demonstrated their love without embarrassment. Difficulties were dealt with together and with God. They expressed their mutual feelings through their actions – by helping each other, caring for one another, and by wanting to "ease" the other person's burdens and pain.

Love toward God was demonstrated by keeping the Ten Commandments and with a terrific respect – constantly remembering the Final Judgment, and carefully honoring all things Holy for worshiping God. The esteem toward God's gifts was simply unheard of –bread was marked with the Sign of the Cross before it was sliced; before baking, every loaf of bread was engraved with a deep cross. Even the smallest crumb that fell onto the floor was lifted with honor and then kissed.

I was often awakened from my sleep by the whispered prayers of my father, who did not kneel to pray, but rather, walked back and forth while praying. My mother knelt with us and taught us to pray while kneeling. My grandmother, on the other hand, prayed constantly; at all times of the day she could be found kneeling somewhere in a doorway or in the corner of a room. My grandfather, a very big and strong man was always more restrained. They had an unusual respect for priests and were very generous to the Church. My grandparents, as well as, my parents accepted all the children that God bestowed upon them.

Growing up, I knew there was a purpose to my life – first, to be the best in school, keeping in mind the perspective of my future life, more than likely within a family. I knew I was responsible for choosing a partner for life, that I could not be rash, though I was aware that I had to pray even harder to make a good choice. I was vigilant when observing a man's behavior, customs and morality.

Beata (married 36 years)

Family was something natural, though not always easy – we worked together to overcome obstacles; we each had our own special place, as well as our own problems that everyone usually knew about...

Krzysztof (married 23 years)

My parents were the best teachers I had. They were wonderful parents, who passed on admirable religious values, traditions, as well as, the holiness and the indissolubility of marriage. My mother was the best role model for me.

Dorota (married 8 years)

In my family home, there was always a normal division: mom, dad and the children. Our grandmother also lived with us. The boys, following the example of our father, knew that their future responsibility was to have a family, work to support it and ensure that meals and prayer were a family activity. Sunday was always a day of rest from work and a day to attend church with the entire family. We did not have to date in secret, but instead we brought our girlfriends home, so that our parents could get to know them.

Stanislaw (married 27 years)

I come from a family with many children in which two things were emphasized: faith and mutual respect. Although we did not have many discussions about these topics with my parents, for me, they always served as an ideal example to follow.

Elizabeth (married 24 years)

My vision for marriage was shaped at home as I watched my parents. All their positive examples were accepted by me naturally, though there were negative examples as well. The undignified behavior of my father – stemming from his alcohol addiction – toward my mother, clearly taught me how I could never be in the future. Paradoxically, those negative examples confirmed an inner determination for me to never repeat the same mistakes in my relationships with my future wife and children.

Slawek (married 23 years)

Marriage was always seen as something special in our family. The example I received from my parents was wonderful – a model of happy, loving relations. As I grew up, I was open to all vocations and even seriously considered a calling to be a nun, however, in my heart there was always a desire to marry and have a big family. I am indebted to my parents for this.

Angela (married 21 years)

I came from a traditional Catholic family, where marriage was to be a union of the husband and wife for life. I prayed daily for a good husband for a number of years.

Helena (married 34 years)

[I had] a good example of a loving family. I was very blessed!

Mike (married 25 years)

My mother died 3 months before I met my future wife. My father lived very far away. I lived with two of my younger brothers. There was not much preparation through my family.

Oram (married 10 years)

My Engagement

During our engagement, we planned our journey together. We talked a lot about what we did not want to have in our future family and how things should be. Very often, we participated in Holy Mass together.

Otylia

Practically speaking, we really did not have a typical "engagement". Since I was only a 17 years old girl, I was not completely aware of what the relationship was really all about. My husband, who was five years older than me, loved me very much. He believed that I would mature and we would live long and happy lives together. I became pregnant after a year, which was a surprise to our parents. We believed, however, that if we entrust our marriage to God, somehow everything would work itself out. From the moment we said "yes" to God, we have been grateful for the gift of the marriage He gave us.

Teresa and Jozef

We met through the youth group at our Church. Our engagement lasted over a year. This was a time of being fascinated with one another, teaching each other and getting to know one another; discussing (...) our expectations and planning our future together.

Ryszard and Joanna

Not everyone realizes that the decision to enter into marriage is one of the most important decisions we make during our earthly existence. Somehow, God arranged it so that at the moment when we make this decision, we are often too young and immature to make the decision properly. We often say we are getting married because that we love him or her. Yet this love is usually not a mature, enduring kind of love. Rather, it is the state of "falling in love" of the soul, which is worth experiencing, but passes quickly. Anyone who has ever been in love knows what it is all about. It is something that I personally look back on with nostalgia and affection. A person is then willing to "move mountains" for the other person. We do not see any flaws of the other person, we would do anything for him and we are ready to make any sacrifice in order to be together. However, for most of us, as I have learned, this emotion last very briefly and passes quickly. Usually, soon after being married, our eyes open and we begin to see the other person's faults. Then, very often, the marriage experiences a crisis. How and if we make it through this crisis is most important.. Many marriages work things out; however, just as many end in divorce.

Katarzyna (married 18 years)

I am among those, who already have the wonderful time of engagement and waiting for my Sacramental Marriage behind me. In those days, the wedding had two parts: the civil contract and later, the real vows. I am among those who walked down the aisle with my head held high, pure, in love and so sure that we were offering ourselves to God, that joy expanded within us like a balloon being filled with hot air. I told everyone then and now, and will continue to do so that it is not a problem to be faithful and pure before marriage. I know what I am talking about! My wife and I dated for four years before marriage. This was not wasted time, but time spent on what God planned for us. It was a time to get to know one another and our families, to understand our weaknesses and mistakes, to eliminate our faults and unacceptable behaviors, a time to plan our lives together, as well as, a beautiful time for parties and church. Time to fall in love. Always, wherever I am, whether with young people or old, I like to talk about preparing for the Sacrament of Marriage, from the purely human - male and female - aspect. I tell everyone it is not true that you have to follow a trend. It is not true that society requires it. It is not true that it is impossible to remain pure for so long. You can do it, you can do it, and again - you can do it! And it's worth it! Worth it a hundred times over! I know because I went through it myself! Nobody is going to convince me otherwise, that things should be different because times have changed! This is no great discovery. Just follow the path God meant for you since He doesn't make mistakes and has foreseen everything.

The reason I write so much, is that, Father, you have hit it right on the nose! This kind of book is more important than you can imagine. I myself, through my contacts, discussions and meetings can do very little to tell people what is worth doing, but this book can reach many people.

Stanislaw (e-mail)

That which I considered an engagement ended suddenly and unexpectedly – meaning? But that which I did not expect continues to this day - as a marriage.

Krzysztof

I met my husband during the summer vacation after my second year at college. We were students at the same school. I did not experience the time before we were married as a time of engagement. We both knew we wanted to be married, but we wanted to finish our studies. We did not promise each other anything before then, and we did not become closer in any way that the 10 Commandments forbid.

Beata

My engagement was too short (only a few months), which made it impossible for me to get to know my future husband well enough.

Dorota

It lasted four years. It was a time to really get to know our families and each other. From the beginning, we had one clear assumption: sex was reserved only for marriage. Keeping to this was not a problem. We tried to put ourselves in many different situations and point out to each other our mistakes; we tried to eliminate unwanted habits.

Stanislaw

My husband and I were married after only five months. We were both 25 years old and had many other relationships behind us, but it did not take long for us to figure out that we should be together forever.

Elzbieta

When I encountered the love of my life, I tried to keep a promise I made to myself as a young man: to never, in anyway, hurt my beloved. I believe that with God's help, I have been successful. We experienced our engagement as a true retreat before marriage, and praying, attending liturgies and participating in pilgrimages together were proof of this. Along with many of our friends, we took up the challenge of the difficult - though possible to achieve - demand to upholding the ethics of premarital love. Karol Wojtyla's call to chastity and beautiful love as well as Pope John Paul II's later directives, helped us enormously with this decision.

Slawek

My engagement was a joyful time of waiting for the Sacrament of Marriage. We spent a lot of time preparing for the Holy Mass, selecting the songs that would be sung, the readings, and so on. The wedding reception was a formality which was joyful, but served only as a gift to our guests. We concentrated on the celebrating the Holy Mass.

Angela

I met my husband when I was 24 years old and married him at 26. We were engaged for about four months. We were living in two different cities at the time.

Helena

[It lasted] eight months – [though it was] supposed to have been ten months, but we moved it so that Brenda's mom could make it. She didn't. She passed away five months before our wedding.

Mike

Our engagement lasted about six months. I met my wife three months before we were engaged. During our engagement, we bought a house where I lived. My wife was from a town far away. We met in a bar that was near my work. We did not live together in our home... until we were married. Though my wife did not practice any religion, she had no qualms about becoming a Catholic. During our engagement, she took classes and about a month or two before we were married, she became a Catholic.

Oram

The Marriage Preparation Course

The marriage teachings were a series of meetings (I can't remember how many) that really impacted us, but the lectures were very general and somewhat official.

Otylia

Taking under consideration the circumstances of our engagement, there was, of course, no thought of any courses.

Teresa and Jozef

We did not participate in a marriage preparation course.

Ryszard and Joanna

Because I did not live near my parish during the time before we were married, I rarely participated in the teachings, which took place once or twice a month. However, in the University town that I lived, I attended the student chapel but did not participate in a parish life. I don't even know whether or not they offered any marriage preparation courses. Before the wedding, no one ever asked that I complete any course.

Beata

I did not participate in any marriage preparation course, which I consider as a great loss. If we had participated, maybe I would have discovered more about my husband's way of thinking.

Dorota

As far as premarital classes are concerned, it would be good if the priests and lay people, who lead these teachings (if not on their own, then perhaps from higher up), would be obliged to take them seriously not to "blow them off". Unfortunately, I have heard many opinions of participants who sat through the required hours only to say it was "a waste of time".

Stanislaw (e-mail)

It was 1980, and the course took place in the church and parish hall. The priest spoke briefly about holiness in Marriage and about the Sacraments, and at other times, lay people gave lectures about the legal aspects of the marriage institution. A retired nurse talked about fertility, natural family planning methods, pregnancy, childbirth and raising children. Not a lot was said about mutual responsibilities or the different way in which men and women view the world.

Stanislaw

Even the best lectures will not help, if we do not take the right lessons from our family homes.

Elizabeth

When I was young, I happened to be very involved in my parish church. When the time came to do a preparatory course for the Sacrament of Marriage, the pastor at the time (I think as a way to "reward" us) excused us from attending the course. Of course, at the time we were elated, but after a couple of years together, we came to understand that this was a mistake on the part of our beloved pastor. We figured out a lot of things on our own, but I think it took greater effort. We should not (today we know) excuse young people from listening to the advice of older, more experienced and faith-filled instructors, who may be able to increase our awareness of various concepts, states or threats to married life. From the perspective of our lengthy marriage, I see the need to give more attention to young men in order to preparing them to be good husbands and fathers. We are, after all, placed at the highest level of responsibility for our loved ones.

Slawek

We were married at a German parish (in Canada), where we met, and which was a part of our family tradition, but we did not have our preparation there. We took the marriage preparation courses at my parish, but there was nothing special touched us there. We discussed the basics... but there was nothing you could "sink your teeth into." It is a shame that no program like Fr. Corapi's *Catechism of the Catholic Church* was available. Looking back, I see how much we lost in those first few years because we lacked in knowledge of our faith, and especially the Sacrament of Marriage.

Angela

My marriage preparation course was once a week for over six or seven weeks at the parish where we got married with about nine or ten other people. The priest participated in some of the sessions. I needed it!

Helena

We met several times with Father Steven Stinson (God rest his soul). [He] made Brenda feel welcomed at the Sacred Heart Engagement Encounter Weekend in Mississauga.

Mike

Before we got married, my wife and I regularly attended Sunday Mass together.

Oram

Being Human in my Marriage

We always try to remember that whether husband or wife, son or daughter, first of all, we are all human beings. Therefore we each have our own individuality, as well as, our own merits and faults. Sometimes it is very difficult, but you have to know how to allow the other person to develop their "humanity" to his or her fullest potential.

Otylia

Knowing that, as a man and a woman we are very different, helps us to mutually enrich each other. Our differences enrich our emotions, often allowing us to make new and wonderful discoveries in our spouse. Thanks to our mutual support, we can develop ourselves while retaining our own identities.

Teresa and Jozef

To be human in a marriage means to put others and their needs before your own. To try to be understanding and patient; learn to talk to one another. This means accepting your own weakness and knowing how to entrust your problems to God. It means knowing how to ask your spouse for help and accepting whatever assistance he or she offers you.

Ryszard and Joanna

I have been married for 18 years. A lot has changed through the years. Today my husband and I are not the same couple we were 18 years ago. We have both changed physically and psychologically. My husband has many good characteristics. He provides for his family, is a good father, a solid man, a hard worker and is trustworthy. That is quite a lot. However, on a psychological level, or in other words, in the spiritual sphere, we are strangers. My husband is not my soul mate. He gives me very little spiritual support. Years, troubles and everyday life have made him into a rough, somewhat bitter person, about whom one cannot say he is pleasant or easy to get along with. He responds negatively, or passive aggressively to many situations. He feels most comfortable when he is alone, in front of his computer, when nobody bothers him or wants anything from him. Many insignificant things can set him off; he is often in a bad mood. Generally speaking, he presents a negative attitude to the world and his surrounding reality. Today, from the perspective of time, I believe that one of the reasons my husband is this way, is because of me. I believe that I didn't know how to show my husband love, and this lack of love was and is the reason that he is rough and bitter. In the past, I did not have the maturity and knowledge that I have now.

Katarzyna

My marriage and children born into it are my whole life. My career and some other successes, such as my education, are simply additional "adornments" – my husband and children are proud of my accomplishments. I express love for my family by creating a warm atmosphere, pleasant aromas, enough nourishment and tasty meals, and by ensuring them a good level of education. I comfort my spouse and children when they are suffering and rejoice with them in their joys.

My days are filled with work and I recognize myself becoming more and more like my grandmother as my days are filled with beloved prayer.

Beata

With great sadness, I must confess that in my marriage I often feel like an object, not a person.

Dorota

Most important is faithfulness. Not a feigned loyalty, but a real trust and my own faithfulness – the kind that does not fear any temptation. My wife is not only the mother of my children; she is also a partner and friend. The words of the vows we exchanged are my motto: "I vow to you my love, faithfulness and marital honesty, and that I will not leave you until death". I take responsibility for these words every day of our lives together.

Stanislaw

Unfortunately, people do not always deserve to be categorized as human. We are lucky enough to belong to those whose love and respect for one another do not allow us to lose faith in humanity.

Elizabeth

I try to realize myself as a man, husband and father, in order to give our children the best possible example. Will this be successful? Surely, in part, but there is still much to do: it is difficult to be a good person to everyone. I try to remember about my joint responsibility for those closest to me, so as to be deserving of eternal life.

Slawek

Before we got married, we discussed who we would be. We would not be Hoffbauers like Mike's parents or Wenzels like Angela's parents. We had to take some ideals from both our homes, but we kept discussing, criticizing and changing them until we made them our own. Somehow it was important for us to sculpt our own path, completely our own, not a reflection of the old way.

Angela

As in any other interaction, I must be true to myself, honest and show respect to my husband with the understanding that he is different from me. Accept him as he is. Support him in his interests and endeavors. Yet, remember that neither of us are perfect!

Helena

We all make mistakes. Since there are two people, that means twice as many human errors. [We] have to be forgiving!

Mike

A way to change yourself as a person after marriage is to constantly think about the feelings of the other person. Step into her feelings and thoughts; care for someone; be more responsible. After the birth of our first child, I began to feel like a lion that takes care of his family. I had to encompass everyone with my care. I had to be a leader for all of us – all six of us.

Oram

Dialog in my Marriage

It is not always easy. Sometimes it seems that "golden" silence is the best answer, but not in a marriage or a family. We try to talk to one another about everything that brings joy or pain, especially when it is something we may not be aware of ourselves.

Otylia

When we were newly married, each of us wanted to be heard. As in many marriages, we fought to be understood, or rather, to have our own way. Afterwards, however, we came to understand that good communication is the basis for true development in marriage. We try to be open to conversation and reveal our true feelings.

Teresa and Jozef

It is very difficult to talk to my husband, especially since he was brought up differently than I. He has a somewhat different approach to the role of women in a marriage, hanging on firmly to the traditional Polish viewpoints that women should do certain tasks in the house (like our grandmothers and mothers did). Then our talks often end in crying, frustration and resignation. There are people who must have silence in order to rest and unwind in the house, while others need to have the radio turned on because they don't like the quiet. Respecting and knowing your spouse is a form also of dialog. This is the ability to put someone else's needs before your own. You cannot change and you should not try to change a man, and those women who plan to change their men after they marry, will quickly find out that it is rather impossible. It is possible, however, regardless of how old fashioned his ideas are, to raise your children in a way that better reflects life in current society, for example, you can teach your son to cook, do laundry and vacuum. You can teach your daughter how (...) to use a hammer, how to mow the lawn and so on. Life is full of surprises and you never know what awaits you. One should talk often and calmly about these things with your children and spouse. This is not about forcing your opinions onto anyone, because that has nothing to do with dialog in your family, but rather, will turns into a monolog that your spouse will simply tune out.

Ryszard and Joanna

Fortunately, in the last couple of years, I have been able to get my hands on some books, probably through the Providence of God, that completely changed the way that I understand marriage and gave me a new perspective on the essence of my problems. First of all, I stopped looking at my marriage from the point of view "what's in it for me?" because as it turns out, there is nothing in it for me expect for the suffering connected to my husband's bad moods. I began to look at things from the point of view: "What can I give of myself to the other person?" This change had an enormous effect on the development of our relationship. In one moment, I moved from the position of "offended victim" to "serving" the other person. I try to give as much as I can of myself, without expecting anything in return. I try to ease his bad moods, provide comfort when he is worried, and help ease the tension and anger. I observed that by responding to anger with anger and hurt with hurt I gained nothing. Actually it was quite the opposite: the pain, anger and other negative emotions multiplied and grew into giant proportions, encompassing and destroying both of us. Gentleness, understanding and tolerance from my part, on the other hand, cause the anger and sour moods to melt away and disappear somewhere. This approach is not easy and requires complete spiritual training, but it gives excellent results. Bringing to life the teachings of Christ, who says: "Love your enemies...", is probably the most difficult thing Christ asks a person to do here on earth. He wants us to like what is not likable and love what is not lovable, not only in marriage, but in our contacts with people in general. After all, what counts in this life on earth, is not how much money we have, what kind of car we drive, what kind of house we live in, how many degrees we have, but rather, who we are as people and how much good we have done for others, "even the least of my brothers", as Christ calls them. This is why it is important to dry tears, comfort the distressed, hug those in sorrow, have compassion for the suffering, and forgive faults "not seven times, but seventy-seven times..."

Katarzyna

It is difficult, but very helpful; it often turns to arguing.

Krzysztof

Dialog in my marriage practically does not exist, because it is difficult to talk to someone who believes he is always right and know everything better.

Dorota

At the beginning we each had our own "sweet secrets", but after many years we came to understand that we cannot have our own "secret worlds". We try to talk about every important matter, including those that pertaining to us directly and those regarding how to raise our children. We take great care to have joint meals and discussions with our children. We try to not interfere too much in their adult lives, but we always must and want to have time to talk with them.

Stanislaw

My husband is very sparse with his words, but this is very good, since there were the unnecessary words that might have been regretted were never spoken. Even without many words, we understand each other very well.

Elzbieta

Dialog is decidedly the most indispensable way we show our love for one another in our marriage. We try to talk about everything in such a way that no subject that is taboo.

Slawek

We always had dialog in our marriage, maybe even too much! Through my work, I took a course in communication and I implemented it out first in our marriage. We probably never had enough time for anything, since we spent so much time talking. I never believed in hiding things under the rug, and my mother-in-law once said that it is not healthy to go to bed when angry with one another. We try to practice this wisdom.

Angela

[We] must be open, speak the truth, listen to the other, be ready to compromise in most decision making. Forgiveness and love overcome differences in opinions.

Helena

Openly discuss everything. Some things are more delicate than others (i.e. family, friends). Sometimes it is nice to be quiet (both people!!).

Mike

Dialog in our marriage is most often instigated by me. My wife is more passive, while I am the leader and make decisions. I always try to make decisions based on her thoughts and feelings. We discuss serious decisions.

Oram

Sexuality in my Marriage

This is one of the many ways in a marriage to show love, closeness, devotion, unity and being together.

Otylia

Sexuality is a wonderful gift that our Creator has given us. For us, it is a celebration of our marriage which is only complete when it is in accordance with God's plan. We were both the first ones for each other, and for us it is very important that we can now learn from each other on the road of love.

Teresa and Jozef

I think that in our generation, among people our age born in Poland, marital sexual issues are very rarely discussed between spouses. It has a great deal to do with how we were raised by our very traditional parents. It is difficult, because we do not know how to talk about these topics openly with our spouse, and sometimes these issues are still awkward to discuss.

Ryszard and Joanna

Our sexual life was also not very successful. We belong to the small group of couples who did not have sex before they were married. Then it turned out that we were not physically sexually compatible. For me, sex was always associated with physical pain that is sometimes difficult to endure. Sexual intercourse is a very important aspect of every marriage, which in our situation works very much to its disadvantage. Sex and physical intimacy are, especially for men, one of the most important ways of showing love. I think that men believe that women (wives) who avoid sex – do not love them.

Katarzyna

Our active sexual life is behind us. It began right after our church wedding. At the appropriate time, we practiced natural family planning, with the result of two daughters and four sons. All the children who were conceived were born, with just one son who suffered during childbirth and was left mentally disabled and with a defective heart. Unfortunately, he is unable to live independently and will probably depend on assistance from his family for the rest of his life.

Beata

For two years we have not had any sexual relations; before then it was sporadic.

Dorota

We share a room and we share a bed. We do not use anti-conception and we do not need other "help". We do not use unnecessary "restraints", but neither do we have problems handling longer periods of abstinence. We hold to the principle that a married couple may only argue until the sun goes down.

Stanislaw

This is a very important element in a marriage, but not the only one. As long as we love each other, even in this area, as in every other one, we can find a common language, as we have for the last 24 years. We did not have a problem regulating ourselves according to the cycle.

Elzbieta

Our behavior in this area is a result of the right kind of preparation before marriage, based on the teachings of the Church. Respecting and fully accepting the natural way of planning for children, based on Pope Paul the VI's encyclical *Humanae Vitae*, we see the great gift and meaning of our intimate sexual life. This particular expression of our love is realized in accordance with the will of the Creator. I believe that living with the mentality to fully respect the laws of nature, through especially respecting your wife, is one of the guarantees of a long lasting and happy marriage.

Slawek

We believe that sexuality is a gift from God and is a very intimate and personal way to share ourselves with each other. An even deeper blessing is the gift of a child, who we respect as being given to us by God. In high school, I had a course in Natural Family Planning and we always practiced it. Here, communication is imperative. Abstinence is also an integral and healthy, as well as, important part of our relationship. I believe that we appreciate each other more because of it. The most important and unifying aspect of our relationship is that the sharing of our faith is greater than the sharing of our bodies.

Angela

Physical closeness is an excellent bond that makes the husband and wife one – united for life. There is no place for such affection with others. Sex is a unique expression of love.

Helena

You will learn over time – how to please the other person and vice versa, and when not to bother them!

Mike

Sexuality in our marriage is very strong in every aspect. Our love for one another and our giving of ourselves is endless.

Oram

Holiness in my Marriage

We make an effort for our marital road to lead us and our children to God, or in other words, to holiness. This means attending Holy Mass together, prayer and honest discussions about the subject of our faith. We feel very secure on "our road" to holiness.

Otylia

We are both aware that the Sacrament of Marriage is a gift and the way to holiness. When we said "I do" to one another, we invited God into our lives, we know that only thanks to Him we can become better.

Teresa and Jozef

It occurs that my husband is the one who ensures that there is time for Holy Mass on Sunday. I don't mean that he forces me to participate, but even when I have a bad day, the weather is awful, and a trip to Church is a four hour affair... I would not even consider mentioning that "maybe we won't go", because I know that such a thought would not even enter into his mind. Praying together or saying the Rosary is also motivational. Religion is a very personal and private thing. If you meet your future spouse at a bar, presenting yourself as a religious person may be difficult. Sometimes we don't know how to bring up this topic during a conversation. If we meet at Church, the situation is a very clear from the beginning. There are no doubts. With the passage of time, our relationship with God has deepened, developed and become not as private. We now know how to talk about the way we pray and why, and we know that when we are faced with a difficult day, praying about it together will bring relief and help.

Ryszard and Joanna

Being with my husband has taught me respect and tolerance of other people. Thanks to the experiences I accumulated in my marriage, often very bitter experiences, I became more patient, understanding and more sensitive to the needs of other people. I learned not to keep the resentment in my heart and always reach out in reconciliation. I learned to treat my husband, son and entire family as gifts from God, to whom I am grateful. I understood that God united us so that we could support each other and help one another in difficult times.

Katarzyna

We take our example from the homes of our grandparents and parents as we continue to preserve the Polish traditional celebrations. We live the Sacraments and use the Sacramentals and all of our children are faithful to the Church. We pray together before meals, up to three times a day. Personally, I try to participate in daily Holy Mass whenever I can.

Beata

I focus on [holiness] in my prayers and in my mind when I am experiencing difficulties.

Krzysztof

Marriage, for me, is holiness, being united by God. As spouses, we are supposed to move towards holiness together, completing each other, so that we can become like the image and likeness of God.

Dorota

Going to Holy Mass together, praying together, reminding each other about regular Confession, and mostly, whenever possible, receiving Holy Communion. When the children were little, they always went with us to Church. This bore fruit so that our adult children now take an active part in the special church celebrations during Advent and Lent.

Stanislaw

Holiness is a concept that is so very unreachable. Although we see our marriage as a grace given to us by God, we are still imperfect people. In our family, Sundays and all Holy days are always days of the Lord and we would never consider neglecting Holy Mass or important liturgies. However, in order to educate three growing children, every other day of the week is very busy.

Elzbieta

I have a wonderful wife, who is already — according to me — a holy person. I simply try to become better and better.

Slawek

Holiness is something I never thought about when I was young. Through many years of marriage, I felt the grace of God and the wisdom of my husband, who is 8 years older than I am... Only later did I realize that I lost a chance at holiness through the vocation of my marriage and in raising my children. I saw a video by Fr. Corapi about the Sacrament of Marriage and then the idea of holiness achieved through this vocation became clear. I wish I had seen this video during my marriage preparation course. Our mission is not just to bring ourselves, but also our spouses and children onto the road to holiness which leads to the eternal home in Heaven.

Angela

We took formal vows to each other in front of a priest and others, and asked God for His blessing in the Sacrament of Marriage. It is sacred and our commitment to each other has never been broken!

Helena

[This is] very important. In today's world, everyone is looking for something to believe. How lucky and fortunate we are to already have God in us!

Mike

To always "be hers" (my wife's), on every path. To always remain faithful to her. To try to show her how much she means to me and how grateful I am to have her.

Oram

What it Means to be a Family Person

This is a very complex question. A one sentence reply would be to love, understand, help, serve, support and be there for the family members.

Otylia

To me, the words "family person" are associated with someone who is warm, sincere, attentive, responsible, with someone who does something in life, not to satisfy his own needs or wants, but takes care of his family and their wellbeing first.

Teresa and Jozef

It seems to me that it means to be there for your family. To ensure your family has a good standard of living, care and safety. It also means to have time for your family, your children and spouse. You sacrifice your time to raise your children, solve family problems, and be aware of all matters regarding your family.

Ryszard and Joanna

I understood that my son is not my property, and his achievements and success should not be to satisfy my own unfulfilled dreams or ambitions. Our children are, for us parents, a great gift from God, and our job is to raise them the best way we know how. I trust that God will guide my son according to His Will, that He will help my son achieve an education and career that will be able to serve people and this planet.

Katarzyna

To be a family person means to have the feeling of belonging to a group with which you have blood relations. It is the care and compassion I show towards my relatives, especially those closest to me and those who depend upon me. It means trying to be a good example in life. Unfortunately, I did not succeed in this. I was not able to raise my children to have their own family lives. Of my six children, only one son got married, but he puts off expanding his family. Those who did not have a family, live decent lives, and I do not know why they chose to remain single.

Beata

It means to be responsible, good and understanding - "to be for them and for us".

Krzysztof

It means putting your family first: husband, children and parents; caring for them and caring for the home; ensuring a good religious upbringing, having many conversations, spending a lot of time together, making time for the children, husband and so on.

Dorota

To create a home where we are bound by the principle of "no closed doors" and there is no isolation of ourselves from certain people. Home is where everyone is important and everyone has a place. To have aloes ties with grandparents, family and friends. Joint celebration of holidays, Christmas Eve spent together and visits to each other for no special reason.

Stanislaw

To find, in this busy life, time to talk to one another, at least eat Sunday dinner together, and during the most difficult situations in life, place the concerns and problems of those closest to us above work and other responsibilities.

Elzbieta

It is definitely to be open to every member of the family – those that are closest, but also those who are more distant. It is also, the ability to be able to receive every guest or person in need.

Slawek

To be a family person, it means to have sacrificial love, to be open for the gift of children and to make your family a priority in your life.

Angela

We were blessed with children and consider that to be a great responsibility to nurture, sustain and care for each other in our family.

Helena

Husband – wife – son – daughter – working together for the betterment of the family, yet being as individual as God made us.

Mike

To be a family man is wonderful. First, to be a husband. Then, to have children as the true gifts of God. To be able to love all my four children with the same heart...is absolutely incredible.

Oram

Budgeting in my Marriage and Family

This is about making decisions on an essential issue which affects each person in the family. Therefore, we always make these decisions together and even this completely normal situation, our unity is an expression of our connection and closeness.

Otylia

We both make important financial decisions; we share our money, our faith and our trust in one another.

Teresa and Jozef

There are couples who have separate bank accounts. Not in our marriage. We entered into this relationship with practically nothing and every material possession we own, was achieved together. It is easier in a marriage when both partners deal with the budget, but unfortunately, in our family this role fell to me. This means, that my husband has absolutely no interest in how much money is needed every month for household and other expenses. He believes that he should not have to care or even take an interest in these things, since I manage them. This is the greatest cause of stress and resentment, though not arguments. The psychological responsibility for such an important part of our life together rests on one person. After so many years, I expect for my husband to relieve me of such stressful responsibilities, maybe not for him to take over it completely, but so that he would take an interest and be oriented in the everyday expenses and income of our family as well as I am.

Ryszard and Joanna

The large number of people in our family determines the condition of the budget. My husband, who has a technical vocation, is responsible for our home, the heating and energy bills, the car and other larger expenses. I, whose background is in the humanities, care for the clothes, shoes, additional language lessons, trips, room and board in other cities and all the other needs of the children.

Beata

It is important, when there is something to divide and there is excess...

Krzysztof

Budgeting is necessary, but unfortunately in my marriage, my husband decides about most of the expenses, shopping and so on, and this is why we often have financial problems.

Dorota

Our joint incomes are absolutely available to both of us. The children receive an allowance and this money is never given as a reward for completing chores. We never had the problem that money had to be kept under "lock and key". Regardless of the sum or where the money is left lying around, nobody touches it. Money is treated exclusively as a means to life, and not as something that has value in itself. Most of our expenses are decided together, however, everyday shopping is done by whoever has time and then he or she takes whatever money is needed without having to document it. We trust each other and there have never been any problems.

Stanislaw

We both work, but I spend most of our earned money on everyday expenses; however, my husband and I discuss every bigger expense together.

Elzbieta

All our income and expenses are our joint creation; there is no division as to "my" or "your" money.

Slawek

I observed my parent's budget through many years. After coming from the bank every Friday, they sat down together in the evening and divided the income for whatever was needed, ensuring that everything would balance. My parents did not need any loans for most of the time I lived at home. We never had a lot of money, but it was always enough. We were taught the value of saving money to achieve a goal. This is the model I brought to our relationship. Michael gave me the responsibility for our finances (as it was with my parents) and he was always generous with his belief in my ability to take care of the expenses and budget. All of our money is in one account, and whatever we have belongs to both of us.

Angela

We have lived frugally and have tried not to spend more than necessary for essentials, yet have had family vacations and some entertainment at times.

Helena

In this aspect of financial planning, marriage is like a business. One has to take charge and be responsible for the financial planning, budgeting, short and long term goals.

Mike

I am happy because I received the wisdom which helps me care for our finances and not have to worry about the budget too much in our marriage.

Oram

Preserving Family Traditions and Building Our Own

There are many beautiful traditions, especially here in our "new county", which are a great treasure for us and we try to pass them on to our children. Traditions are a force which strengthen and develop, as well as, enrich our family ties.

Otylia

The traditions that our parents passed to us, we pass on to our own children. However, we try to dig even deeper into their true meanings, and by expanding our knowledge about them, we introduce our own traditions. This enriches our family life. They are so beautiful that we want to cultivate them, believing that our children will pass them on further.

Teresa and Jozef

We try to keep Polish traditions alive during the holidays. Since are both from Poland, our traditions are very similar. I think, however, that bringing in new traditions is very difficult because of our parents, who are even more attached to these Polish traditions than we are; they look at upon every new thing unfavorably.

Ryszard and Joanna

We have kept most of the traditions taken from our family homes and we consider them our own, because we continue to cultivate them.

Beata

Dreams of a pleasant atmosphere – known from stories of the past – but this is created through repetition, returning, remembering.

Krzysztof

Traditions and the Polish language are very important to me, and I preserve the traditions I brought from my family home with such great dedication and determination, so that our children may also carry them on.

Dorota

Holiday traditions, like spending Christmas Eve together, singing carols, having a Christmas tree for Christmas holidays, decorating the house, hosting the priest during parishioner visits after the holidays, breaking of the Blessed Bread with friends and family (a Polish tradition), the blessing the food baskets on Holy Saturday, Adoration at church during Holy Week, birthday presents, name-day celebrations, surprises, and mandatory visits to grandparents.

Stanislaw

My parents raised and educated eight children. We have the great fortune that we all now live in the same city. I cannot imagine the holidays without sharing the Blessed Bread at Christmas, or sharing the food from the blessed basket at Easter with those who are closest to me. Although it is not easy for hosts to fit 30 or so people into an average sized apartment, the atmosphere of these meetings allows for everyone to treat any discomfort as unimportant. In these times, the younger generation, unfortunately, more and more often goes out into the wide world, but they will always return, whenever possible, to spend these most important days of the year with their family. What is most important, however, is that no problems were able to divide us and we can always count on each other's help. I will be very happy if we were able to pass on to our children what we took from our family homes so that one day they will know how to create their own families.

Elzbieta

We try to preserve and cultivate all the traditions we brought from our family homes. We have also created an example of life and spending our holidays and family celebrations without alcohol.

Slawek

We try to uphold our German traditions. Before our youngest of five children had problems with his speech and we needed to take him to a therapist, we spoke to all our children in German and English. Since we needed assistance from outside, it became necessary at that time to only speak English. Nonetheless, we continue to preserve all of our German traditions, especially during Christmastime. We also cook according to our traditions. Our own family tradition is focused around our faith and is built around the Liturgical calendar of the Church, feast days and holy days. This has more meaning to us than the cultural traditions and we feel a very strong need to pass it down to our children.

Angela

Our extended family traditions and gatherings are very important. Christian holidays, nuclear family birthdays and anniversaries are special times to be together.

Helena

Coming from an Italian background, our family is very fortunate to reap the culture, customs and traditions of our heritage. Our own family traditions, we try to keep focused on traditional upbringing and adopt to today's way of life.

Mike

Neither one of us had a tradition. I come from a home where my mother was a Catholic but my father was not. He had a problem with alcohol which destroyed their marriage. My wife also had an even more difficult life. Her mother did nothing to take care of her three children and her father was also an alcoholic. Their marriage ended when she was 14 years old. So our family tradition is this:

1. God and prayer.
2. Love, Love and more Love for one another.
3. Thinking about the feelings of the other person.

Oram

Summary

Alan Loy McGinnis, in his book *Bringing Out the Best in People* (Minneapolis, 1995), lists, at the very beginning, the principles of good team work and mutual motivation to better one. You can easily apply this list to engaged, married, or family relationships.

1. Expect the best from the people you lead.
2. Make a thorough study of the other person's needs.
3. Establish high standards for excellence.
4. Create an environment where failure is not fatal.
5. If they are going anywhere near where you want to go, climb on other people's bandwagon.
6. Employ models to encourage success.
7. Recognize and applaud achievement.
8. Employ a mixture of positive and negative reinforcement.
9. Appeal sparingly to the competitive urge.
10. Place a premium on collaboration.
11. Build into the group an allowance for storms.
12. Take steps to keep your own motivation high.

A marriage that is planned by God the Creator, as a unique union of "two that are one", with the triple assistance of God and people can – with the help of Christ – bring out the best in a husband and wife so that the two can become one. No other marriage – besides the Sacramental one – has such amazing assistance in building this incredible marital union. Both spouses need the living God at every moment of their lives in their common pilgrimage on this earth as a family of God to the Heavenly Family in the House of the Father.

McGinnis, in his list of 12 principles, did not make any mention of the grace that is given to sacramentally married spouses. If, as Pope John Paul II said in his first pilgrimage to his homeland in 1979, a person without Christ is not able to completely understand himself, then how can he understand another person, even he they love her. You cannot measure a person by strictly earthly standards. The human person aspires to something that is beyond time, beyond this earth. A person is more than a union of body and spirit. His reality is unimaginably greater.

Human beings are not only the "image and likeness" of the Creator, but from the times of Jesus Christ, we are His brothers and sisters, saved and adopted in Jesus, the child of God the Father! Married spouses, whose union is planned by God the Creator, will only be completely happy if they live every moment according to His, not only their own (even the most noble), plan!

How many times have we seen a wonderful engaged couple, according to our human "estimations" and how bright their married future seemed to be? Then something happened, something got "stuck" and their married life ended very painfully, or even tragically. Sometimes, when sitting together with the spouses and looking for reasons why their marriage fell apart, we discovered, after a short analysis, that when they walked out of the church on their wedding day, they left Christ behind... in the church. He invited them (or perhaps their parents invited Him) to the celebration of their wedding in church, but they did not even take Him to the wedding feast (of course, it did not take place in Cana, and they had plenty of wine). Maybe they thought they would make it on their own, and He – Christ – would maybe make them uneasy with His presence and evangelical principles. They received the sacrament as a gift, but rejected the realization of this sacramental gift in everyday life. They wrote the history of their own marriage, but without the participation of Jesus and Mary. Their history became a contradiction of the plan Christ had for them. When it was too late, they looked for a scapegoat and blamed the Church for their broken marriage, instead of immediately looking to the Church for answers to their difficulties. Thus, for years after leaving the Church, they did not need the Church to "meddle in their affairs". Now, they do not want to admit that their marital experiment without the Church and without Christ backfired.

We have often met people who are simple, yet so incredibly deep in their spirituality. They, although seemingly imperfect and without little chance of a good marriage, slowly, with prayer from the hearts, allowed their innermost spiritual selves to be "sculpted" by the Best Sculptor-Artist, Christ Himself. They invited Christ not only to their wedding celebrations, but also to remain with them throughout their entire married lives. He was with them throughout joyous and sad times, in health and in sickness, in days of fertility and in days of waiting, in the happy moments of conception and childbirth. Every day, they recognized Him with their minds and loved Him with their hearts through individual meetings and joint prayers. He fed them with his Body and Blood in the Eucharist on Sundays and feast days, and even during the week. He always had time for them, and they for Him, thought they were often very busy. They invited Him to the dinner table and discussions about "what to do and how to make our marriage and family better". He understood their falls and taught them to forgive, and they accepted Him and their mutual forgiving with gratitude. What a fantastically special "marital triangle": husband, wife and Him – Christ (God-Man), always thirsty and ready to develop them in their beautiful, sacrificial marital and family lives! They celebrated their following anniversaries with ever growing gratitude, and with their every growing family, sang songs of thanks to Jesus for his creative and uniting presence within them.

Although after many years they remained (physically) alone at home, though their hair turned silver or became sparse, though they had to lead one another arm in arm to Holy Communion, though later death separated them in body, He was with continuously with them here on Earth and there in Heaven. Those spouses, who left behind their bodies, He greeted as a Friend, and they were WITH HIM again and

TOGETHER WITH GOD IN THE HOUSE OF THE FATHER! What an incredible vision and reality of sacramentally marital life here on Earth and after a physical separation, there in eternity.

How can one not love Christ and the Church for His gift – the Sacrament of Marriage, especially today in a time of almost demonic and perfidious attacks on marriage as a gift of unified life and a man and woman and as the gifts of sacramental husband and sacramental wife!

How can we not love each other as sacramental spouses, feeling and experiencing this unbreakable bond daily in the presence of Jesus and with the help of His Mother! No true love ever dies! Authentic love unties people with God and in God forever!

The comments of sacramentally married spouses in some way paint a splendid mosaic of their joint and sometimes difficult lives in faith and love in Christ. Their reflections, based on personal experiences, are the richness of their internal marital lives which are so closely united with Jesus.

I, as a pastor, personally know some of the respondents to the questionnaire. Their responses are true. May their testimonies bring forth a song of gratitude for them and with them to Christ, who wandered with them on this earthly pilgrimage (often far from their place of birth) to their Heavenly Home. Even more valuable are the testimonies of life in difficulty and unity. Oh, how important it is to offer your married, and later family, lives jointly to Christ and His Mother: the ceremonious beginning of your lives together at the altar as well as the everyday living in a growing family her on earth, and later it is also worth desiring a unified life in the Home of the Father.

A Bit of Humor

Question: What couple shouldn't get married because their marriage won't work?
Answer: She is a mathematician and he is hard to figure out (or vice versa).

Question: Why were Adam and Eve the ideal couple?
Answer: Adam never heard Eve say that she could have married someone else. Eve never heard Adam say that his mom cooks better.

The mother asks, "Daughter, you have been dating him for such a long time. People are already talking about you. Why don't you marry him?" She responds, "Mother, how can I marry him if he does not believe in Hell?" Before the mother reacted, the father lifted his eyes from the newspaper and said, "Don't worry. When he marries you, he'll start to believe."

Wife to husband: "If you were well behaved, you would say something... so that I could take a breath."

While filling out documents, the priest says to the young woman, "Why do you want to marry him so badly? He is a jerk." The woman replies, "Father, all of my friends are jealous that he is so handsome, and I also want something to look at." A few weeks after the wedding, the young wife comes to the priest and says, "You were right, Father, he is a jerk". The priests looked at her and replied, "Well, you wanted something to look at." Both of her eyes were black and blue.

The young groom-to-be asks the priest in the parish office, "How much for the wedding?" The priest replies, "As much as you think your future wife is worth." The young man hands $50 to the priest. "That's too much," the priest says and gives him back $20.

Husband to his wife: "I always have a picture of you in my wallet." "That's lovely, honey," she replies.

"You don't want to ask why?"

"Of course, it's because you love me."

"No, that's not the reason."

"Then tell my why."

"Every time I have a problem, I look at your photo and I tell myself, 'it could have been worse'."

"What is that supposed to mean?"

"Your photo is a little problem. I put is in my pocket. It will not say anything, but I can tell it everything. It's different with you. You won't let me say a word, because you think you're always right."

A young wife prepares the second course in the kitchen while her husband sits at the table and eats soup. Suddenly she hears his loud and nervous shout, "Come here! Look! There is a hair in the soup. Am I supposed to eat it?" She responds calmly, "My dear, why are you so upset? Don't you remember, not long ago before our wedding, you told me you love me so much you could swallow me whole? And you can't even eat this tiny hair?"

"What a wonderful husband you have!"

"Really? If not for the church wedding and this ring, I'd give him to you right now."

A woman complains about the man she marries should remember that she could have caught a better fish if only she had better bait.

In Hollywood, at a 25th wedding anniversary party of a pair of actors, the surprised journalists asked the wife, "Twenty-five years together! Tell us, did you ever think about divorcing him?" "No, never," she replied, "but I've sometimes thought about killing him."

Married couples who claim that in their 25 years together, they never had an argument, either have poor memories or had boring lives.

"Could you tell me, my dear, who you are writing that letter to?" the wife asked her husband.
"Why are you asking me about that?"
"Don't be strange. Do you always have to know everything?"

The following occurred on my train trip from Poznan to Warsaw in 1969. A lady sitting by the window said, "After 25 years of marriage, divorce should be allowed". I question her about the reasons, but finding none, I ask, "Why do you say that?" "Well," she replied, "you can't constantly look at the same picture". Then I tell her, "You know, that picture is different in the morning, different at noon, different in the evening and different at night." She glanced over at me, (I was dressed in French priest style, so she did not know I was a priest), smiled and said, "Sir, you are so young but you already know so much about marriage. You're right!"

A young man asks a Greek philosopher, "Tell me, should I get married or not?" The philosopher replied calmly, "Whatever you do, you will regret it.

Two friends had big problems. Their wives were very sick for a long time. One day, one of them saw the happy face of his friend and asked, "Why are you so happy?"

"I found a young, very smart doctor who cured my wife!"

"Really? How did he do that? I need one like that because my wife is always sick. I've been to many doctors, even overseas, and none have helped her. I don't have any more money."

"We sat in his office and my wife complained about her ailments for about 20 minutes. When she finished, the doctor said, 'I think these are the first signs of...,' and took a very deep breath, then added, 'of getting old.' Since that moment, she never mentioned being sick."

A woman comes to the police station to report that her husband is missing. The policeman asks for a photo of her husband. She takes is from her purse and hands it to the policeman. He looks at it and says, "Do you really want to find him?"

After 65 years of marriage, an ailing wife says to her husband, "My dear, give me that box on the shelf." When the husband gave it to her, she said, "Open it." After he opened it, he saw two dolls and $95,000. Perplexed, he said, "My dear, we never had any secrets from one another. Tell me, where did you get so much money?" She responds, "After the wedding, your mother told me never to argue with you. Instead, I should knit. I chose to make dolls." "There are two here, but where did the money come from?" "From the sale of my dolls over the past 65 years!"

Before the final blessing, the priest said to the newly sacramentally married couple, "Today, you receive the guardian angel. Remember that the angel will fly away, but the guardian will stay."

Suggested Reading

Teachings of the Catholic Church

A Family Perspective in Church and Society. Committee on Marriage and Family, National Conference of Catholic Bishops, [Edition Information: 10th anniversary ed.] Washington, D.C.: U.S. Catholic Conference, c1998.

Catechism of the Catholic Church, Libreria Editrice Vaticana 1997, 2nd ed.
Catholic Marriage Advisory Council, *Preparing Engaged Couples for Marriage,* London, Catholic Marriage Advisory Council [1967].

John Paul II, *Familiaris Consortio,* The Apostolic Exhortation on the Family, L'Osservatore Romano (English Edition), vol. 14, nos. 51-52, (December 21-28, 1981).

John Paul II, *Gratissimam Sane.* Letter to Families. Rome 1994.

John Paul II, *Original Unity of Man and Woman. Catechesis on the Book of Genesis,* Boston, Mass.: St. Paul Editions, c1981.

John Paul II, *Theology of the Body,* September 19, 1979, "The Second Account of Creation: The Subjective Definition of Man," *L'Osservatore Romano* (English Edition), vol. 12, no. 39.

Paul VI, *Humane Vitae.* Encyclical of on the Regulation of Birth, July 25, 1968;

Pontifical Council for the Family, *The family and human rights,* Roma 1999;

Service de préparation au mariage de Montréal. *The Union of Love. A Catholic Marriage Manual for Engaged Couples. Prepared by the Institute for the Preparation of Marriage, Montreal, Canada,* New York, Benziger Bros. [1967].

United States Catholic Conference, *Planning Your Wedding Ceremony,* Washington, D.C. c1990.

United States Catholic Conference, *Making Marriage Work,* Washington, D.C.: c1990.

United States Catholic Conference, *Our Future Together,* Washington, D.C.: c1990.

United States Catholic Conference, *Parenthood,* Washington, D.C. : c1990.

Literature

Abad, Javier, *Marriage. A Path to Sanctity,* Manila: Sinag-Tala Publishers, 2002.

Amodei, Michael, *Marriage and Holy Orders. Your Call to Love and Serve,* Notre Dame, Inc.: Ave Maria Press, c2007.

Antonio, David William, *An Inculturation Model of the Catholic Marriage Ritual,* Collegeville, Minn.: Liturgical Press, c2002.

Aridas, Chris, *Your Catholic Wedding. A Complete Planbook,* New York: Crossroad Pub., 1997.

Barkley Roy, *Journey of faith. Catholic marriage preparation,* Goleta, CA: Queenship Pub. Co., c2002.

Bookar Lisa Darline, *Marriage and marital therapy. International survey with medical research subject directory and bibliography,* Edition Information: 1st ed.: Washington, D.C.: ABBE Publishers Association, 1983.

Bosco Antoinette, *Growing in faith when a Catholic marriage fails: for divorced or separated Catholics and those who minister with them,* Totowa, N.J: Resurrection Press, c2006.

Brinley Douglas E., *Together forever, Gospel perspectives for marriage and family/* Published/Created: Salt Lake City, Utah: Bookcraft, c1998.

Brandt Henry, *Marriage, God's way,* Nashville, Tenn.: Broadman & Holman, c1999.

Cedar-Southworth Donna Marie, *The Catholic marriage wisdom book,* Huntington, Ind. : Our Sunday Visitor, 2000.

Clemens Alphonse Henry, *Marriage and the family, an integrated approach for Catholics,* Englewood Cliffs, N.J., Prentice-Hall, 1957.

Dantec François, *Love is life. A Catholic marriage handbook.* Rev. and adapted by Albert Schlitzer. Foreword by Theodore M. Hesburgh. [Notre Dame, Ind.] University of Notre Dame Press [1963].

Embodied in love. Sacramental spirituality and sexual intimacy. A new Catholic guide to marriage, [Charles A. Gallagher et al.]. New York, NY: Crossroad, 1983.

Fehrenbach, Paul K., *Soul and self. Parallels between spiritual and psychological growth,* New York: Paulist Press, c2006.

Ford, David and Mary, *Marriage as a Path to Holiness. Lives of Married Saints,* [with a foreword by his grace Bishop Kallistos of Diokleia], South Canaan, Pa.: St. Tikhon's Seminary Press, 1994.

Giandurco, Joseph R., *Partners in Life and Love. A Preparation Handbook for the Celebration of Catholic Marriage,* New York: Alba House, c1996.

Gordon, Lori H., *Prepairs. A Guide for Catholic Marriage,* [United States]: 1stBooks, c2002.

Gould, Joseph, *Together: 99 Ways to Save Your Marriage from the Start,* Wilsonville, OR: BookPartners, 1999.

Grunlan, Stephen A., *Marriage and the Family, A Christian Perspective,* Grand Rapids, MI: Zondervan, c1999.

Hamrogue, John, *What Every Catholic should Know about Sex and Marriage,* Liguori, MO: Liguori Publications, 1998.

Hauser, Daniel, *Marriage and Christian Life. A Theology of Christian Marriage,* Lanham, MD: University Press of America, c2005.

Keenan, Alan, Ryan John, *Marriage, a Medical and Sacramental Study,* New York, Sheed and Ward, 1955.

Lawler, Michael G., *Marriage and Sacrament. A Theology of Christian Marriage*, Collegeville, Minn.: Liturgical Press, c1993.

Lawler, Michael G., *Marriage and the Catholic Church. Disputed Questions*, Collegeville, Minn.: Liturgical Press, c2002.

Lawler, Michael G., *Secular Marriage, Christian Sacrament*, Mystic, Conn.: Twenty-Third Publications, c1985.

Lovasik, Lawrence G., *The Catholic Family Handbook. Time-tested Techniques to Help you Strengthen your Marriage and Raise Good Kids*, Manchester, N.H.: Sophia Institute Press, c2000.

Lovasik, Lawrence G., *Catholic Marriage and Child Care*, Boston, Christopher Pub. House [1962]

Lynch, William Albert, *The Catholic Marriage. A Handbook*, [foreword by Richard Cardinal Cushing] London, Corgi, 1968.

Mackin, Theodore, *The Marital Sacrament*, New York: Paulist Press, c1989.

Maida, Adam J., *The Tribunal Reporter. A Comprehensive Study of the Grounds for the Annulment of Marriage in the Catholic Church*, edited by the Canon Law Society of America. Huntington, Ind., Our Sunday Visitor [1970-].

Marriage and the Family. Practical Instructions on the Duties of the Catholic Home, New York, The America Press, 1918.

Marriage and Family Education in Theological Perspective. Pastoral and Practical Implications. Report of Consultation, Milan, Italy 2nd to 7th

November 1979, [Geneva] : Office of Family Education, World Council of Churches, 1980.

Marriage. A Psychological and Moral Approach, New York, Fordham University Press [1965].

Marriage in Christ. The Rite of Marriage, Newly Translated, with an Introduction, by Richard E. Power, [Edition Information: 4th rev. ed.] Collegeville, Minn., Liturgical Press, 1941.

Marriage in the Catholic Tradition. Scripture, Tradition, and Experience, [edited by Todd A. Salzman, Thomas M. Kelly, and John J. O'Keefe], New York: Crossroad Pub. Co., 2004.

Marriage is More than You & Me. Reflections for Engaged Couples Entering Catholic Matrimony, Chicago, IL: ACTA Publications, c1992.

Marshall, John, *Family Planning by the Temperature Method,* London, Catholic Marriage Advisory Council, [1970].

McGraw, Woody, *Marriage According to God's Word. How to Succeed at Marriage,* Crestwood, KY : Trinity House, 1983.
Mihanovich, Clement Simon, *A Guide to Catholic Marriage,* Milwaukee, Bruce Pub. Co., [1963].

Nappi, Rebecca, *101 Questions and Answers on Catholic Marriage Preparation,* New York: Paulist Press, c2004.

Pontifical Council for the Family, *Marriage and Family. Experiencing the Church's Teaching in Married Life,* San Francisco: Ignatius Press, c1989.

Ritvo, Eva C., *Concise Guide to Marriage and Family Therapy*, Washington, DC: American Psychiatric Pub., c2002.

Robinson, Josephine, *Marriage as a Gift. A Catholic Approach*, [Edition Information: 1st North American ed.] Boston, MA: Pauline Books and Media, 2007.

Rubio, Julie Hanlon, *A Christian Theology of Marriage and Family*, New York: Paulist Press, c2003.

Sause, Bernard Austin, *Why Catholic Marriage is Different*, St. Louis, MO, and London, B.: Herder book co., 1937.

Seltz, Gregory, *Marriage and Family*, St. Louis, MO: Concordia Pub. House, c2006.

Shivanandan, Mary, *Crossing the Threshold of Love: A New Vision of Marriage in the Light of John Paul II's Anthropology*, Washington, D.C.: Catholic University of America Press, 1999. xxiv, 324 p.

Siegle, Bernard Andrew, *Marriage According to the New Code of Canon Law*, New York, N.Y.: Alba House, 1986.

The Hatherleigh Guide to Marriage and Family Therapy, New York: Hatherleigh Press, 1996.

Urbine, William & Seifert William, *On Life and Love. A Guide to Catholic Teaching on Marriage and Family*, Mystic, Conn.: Twenty-Third Publications, c1993.

Von Hildebrand, Dietrich, *Marriage: the Mystery of Faithful Love*, Manchester, N.H.: Sophia Institute Press, 1984.

Von Hildebrand, Dietrich, *Love, Marriage, and the Catholic Conscience: Understanding the Church's Teachings on Birth Control,* Manchester, N.H.: Sophia Institute Press, c1998.

Waldman, Anne, *Marriage. A Sentence,* New York: Penguin Books, 2000.

West, Christopher, *Theology of the Body for Beginners: A Basic Introduction to Pope John Paul's II's Sexual Revolution,* West Chester, PA: Ascention Press, 1990.

Wojtyla, Karol, *Love and Responsibility,* San Francisco, CA: Ignatius Press, 1993.

Young, William E., *The What, Why and How of Marriage Annulments,* Liguori, MO: Liguori Publications, 2002.